THE
DEE BRESTIN
BIBLE STUDY SERIES

The
Friendships
of
Women

BIBLE STUDY GUIDE

OVERCOMING THE PAIN
AND RELEASING THE POWER

David C Cook®
transforming lives together

The Dee Brestin Series
From David C. Cook
BOOKS

The Friendships of Women

We Are Sisters

The Friendships of Women Devotional Journal

We Are Sisters Devotional Journal

BIBLE STUDY GUIDES

A WOMAN OF LOVE
Using Our Gift for Intimacy (Ruth)

A WOMAN OF MODERATION
Breaking the Chains of Poor Eating Habits (Topical)

A WOMAN OF FAITH
Overcoming the World's Influences (Esther)

A WOMAN OF CONTENTMENT
Insight into Life's Sorrows (Ecclesiastes)

A WOMAN OF CONFIDENCE
Triumphing over Life's Trials (1 Peter)

A WOMAN OF BEAUTY
Becoming More Like Jesus (1, 2, 3 John)

A WOMAN OF PURPOSE
Walking with the Savior (Luke)

A WOMAN OF WISDOM
God's Practical Advice for Living (Proverbs)

A WOMAN OF WORSHIP
Praying with Power (10 Psalms with a music CD)

A WOMAN OF HEALTHY RELATIONSHIPS
Sisters, Mothers, Daughters, Friends (Topical)

A WOMAN OF HOSPITALITY
Loving the Biblical Approach (Topical)

THE FRIENDSHIPS OF WOMEN BIBLE STUDY GUIDE correlates with THE FRIEND-SHIPS OF WOMEN

THE FRIENDSHIPS OF WOMEN BIBLE STUDY GUIDE
Published by David C. Cook
4050 Lee Vance View
Colorado Springs, CO 80918 U.S.A.

David C. Cook Distribution Canada
55 Woodslee Avenue, Paris, Ontario, Canada N3L 3E5

David C. Cook U.K., Kingsway Communications
Eastbourne, East Sussex BN23 6NT, England

David C. Cook and the graphic circle C logo
are registered trademarks of Cook Communications Ministries.

ISBN 978-0-7814-4456-9

Interior Design: Nancy L. Haskins
Cover Design: Greg Jackson, Thinkpen Design, llc
Cover Photo: 2006 © Imagestate

Printed in the United States of America
First Edition 2006

2 3 4 5 6 7 8 9 10

102407

Contents

Acknowledgments 5

Introduction 6

Special Instructions for Preparation 7

Special Instructions for Discussion 8

1. From Girlhood On, Gifted for Intimacy 9

2. Unleashing Our Gift 19

3. The Darker Side of Being Crazy-Glued 33

4. Relational Idolatry 47

5. Naomi: A Female Job 59

6. Ruth: A Woman Friend .74

7. The Risk of Love 86

8. Best Friends 98

9. Unfailing Love 109

10. Roses and Alligators 121

11. God Knows Our Needs Better than We Do 135

12. The Mentor Relationship 148

13. Reflections of Christ 159

Leader's Helps 168

To Patti, Lorinda, Lee, Shell, & Jean

One by one, God brought each of you into my life
when I was a young believer.

For more than twenty-five years, you have loved me
with the love of the Lord.

How I Thank God For:

The team at David C. Cook in Colorado Springs

Who listen to the Lord, to each other, and to me.

My staff at Women's Friendships Ministries

Christy, Jill, Cari, Sandi, Karen. A particular thanks to Christy for so vulnerably sharing her story of relational idolatry.

My annual and perennial friends

Some of you, like annual flowers, have faded out of my life—yet you brought beauty, and I remember you with thankfulness. Some of you are perennials—you have been there in season and out. You have brought warmth, comfort, and spiritual strength to me—and I never stop thanking God for you.

My e-mail prayer team

Thank you. Thank you.

To Steve

I miss you more than I can say, but as I reflect on your life I am in awe at your unselfishness in encouraging me in ministry. How blessed I was by your presence, how blessed I am by your legacy.

Introduction

In 1987 the first edition of *The Friendships of Women* was released. The response was overwhelming. Women wrote saying Dee had touched a cord so deep, and sometimes, so buried, that they finally understood their own hearts. Over a million copies were sold.

Dee attributes the success to God's mercy in revealing secrets to her from Scripture. As she studied three models, a pattern began to emerge—a pattern that, if practiced, can help prune away the pain and release the power in women, the power of their God-given gift for intimacy. Dee writes:

> *I am so excited now, to provide women with an in-depth Bible study on the subject of* The Friendships of Women. *Friendship is not a fluffy topic, for God has used women mightily to bring warmth and redemption to a cold and hurting world. Consider, for example, that a whole book in the Bible is named after Ruth, whose name means "a woman friend." It is as if God is saying, "I know how I created you as a woman—now, let me show you a woman who knew how to use that gift."*

> *We will study other models as well, and as we do, a pattern will emerge, a pattern that, if practiced, will change your life.*

Do you need to also read *The Friendships of Women*? It will definitely augment your study if you do, and you will have a chance each week to reflect on your readings. But if you are a nonreader, you will survive without it, for this study is complete in itself.

Special Instructions for Preparation

Recently I began a Bible study in my home and announced there would be homework. One woman, as she was leaving, said, "Pray for me—I hate homework!"

The next week she arrived smiling. "It wasn't so bad! I just told myself I couldn't watch television until I had it done, and I did it. I even liked doing it."

Those who have been successful in establishing a daily habit of meeting with God find it helps to choose the same time and place each day. Before you begin, ask God to speak to you personally. What could be more exciting than having the living God speak to you? Often the fifth day of each week is the important wrap-up day, so be sure you get to it.

Because this Bible study emphasizes our horizontal relationships, you will also have an exercise that will help you with your vertical relationship with God. Over the course of the study you will pray through one of the most beloved (and longest) psalms: Psalm 119. It is important for us to pray freely and spontaneously, but it is also important for us to learn to pray Scriptures, so that our prayers do not become shallow. Read a verse, reflect on it, and then respond to it.

If you are really stumped on a question, you might find the answer in the back in Leader's Helps, or simply wait for the study and get a little help from your friends.

Special Instructions for Discussion

In the discussion, be sensitive to the Spirit. The naturally talkative need to exercise control. Are you speaking up many times? Hold back so the shy have time to gather courage and speak up. Are you naturally shy? Star the questions where you might share, and then ask God for the courage to speak up.

Stay on target in the discussions. These lessons can be discussed in ninety minutes. If you don't have that much time, you have two options:

A. Divide the lessons, and do the prayer exercise both weeks.

B. Do the whole lesson, but discuss half the questions.

Follow the instructions for group prayer at the close of each lesson. If the idea of praying aloud terrifies you, take heart. You will be led into this gently. You will also cluster with just a few women so it will not be so intimidating. It will not only get easier, but also become one of the best parts of meeting together. There is power when we pray together. One of the threads you will discover is the importance of taking risks—risk making yourself vulnerable and ask for what is really on your heart. Another thread you will discover is unfailing love—and part of that is being trustworthy with confidences.

One

From Girlhood On, Gifted for Intimacy

I cannot count the number of times my heart has been lifted by a woman friend. A heartfelt hug, an e-mail telling me why I am special, a surprise gift of a bracelet I admired when I was with her...

My husband rarely was loved that way by his male friends. *Newsweek* columnist Elliot Engel reflected, "It seems, in our society, that you've got to have a bosom to be a buddy." It certainly comes more naturally to women than to men to confide, console, and connect. When God knit us together in our mother's womb, He created us to be female. Even science today concedes that our differences are much deeper than physical—etched in our very DNA is a gift for intimacy.

When God gives you a gift, He expects you to use it well. Every single one of God's gifts: food, sex, and yes, friendship—has been misused. In our depravity we turn gifts into gods, clinging to them too tightly, abusing them, turning what was intended to be a blessing into bondage. God in His mercy has given us instructions on how to use His gifts well, according to the Manufacturer's instructions. His good gift of food is to be eaten in moderation. His delightful gift of sex is to be kept within marriage. What about friendship? Are there instructions there as well?

Absolutely. In this guide you will study three generations of friendship:

Ruth and Naomi
David and Jonathan
Mary and Elizabeth

I include a male model in this guide because, first, David and Jonathan, as two rare right-brained males, can teach even women a few things about friendship. I also want to include them because, as we study three models, a pattern begins to emerge. If you have ever knit a scarf or worked a weaving loom, you know the delight you feel when the same design begins to repeat. But when it happens in God's Word, you know God is saying something important to you. In the case of friendship, the principles emerging, if applied, will increase the power and reduce the pain of your wonderful gift for intimacy.

Pass around an e-mail, address, and phone sign-up. The facilitator should make copies of the list to hand out next week. Tape or staple the list in your book when you get it, as you'll need it!

DAY 1

Getting to Know You

WARMUP

(If a woman is uncomfortable being "put on the spot," she can simply say "Pass," and go to the next woman.)

Tell your name and a sentence about yourself. What do the friendships of women mean to you? What are you looking forward to in this group?

The opening introductions are vital. Read them carefully.

1. Comment on what stood out to you from the:

    A. Introduction (p. 6)

    B. Special instructions for preparation and discussion (p. 7)

    C. This week's opening (above)

2. The principles in God's Word can transform your friendships. Before you begin (for you will look back at this question at the close), in what ways are your friendships with women painful? In what ways have you also experienced comfort, strength, and genuine help?

DAY 2

. . . .

Appreciating the Power

This year I lost my fifty-nine-year-old husband, the love of my life, to colon cancer. If ever I have appreciated the friendships of women, it is this year. During Steve's illness, my friends prayed fervently for his healing. My dear friend Jill, who also happens to be a nurse, helped me care for Steve when he was suffering. When God chose to take Steve home, my friends rushed to my side with tears, gifts of food, letters of compassion, and promises of unfailing love. Lorinda and Lee flew across the country. Patti would wake in the night and pray for me. Jean would call me daily to check on me. Lorma would have my fatherless daughters over to love on them. This fall, as I approach the first anniversary of his death, Kathy Troccoli decided I needed a lift from the sadness and flew out to help me redecorate my cottage so that I could "live in beauty because beauty restores the soul."

We have a gift, and when that gift is used in obedience to the Holy Spirit, it has enormous power to bless. As a glimpse of what is to come, today you are going to look at a few passages from the book of Ruth to see how these women loved each other. Ruth's name means "a woman friend." Isn't it wonderful that there is a book of the Bible named after "a woman friend?" To me it is an affirmation from God: "I created you, as a woman, with a gift for intimacy. Now, let me show you a woman who used her gift well."

Read Ruth 1 as an overview.

3. What are some of the losses Naomi suffered in the opening seven verses? List as many as you can.

4. What are some ways Ruth demonstrated her love and respect to Naomi? List as many as you can.

5. Think about a time when you were suffering and a friend demonstrated her love to you. What did she do that you particularly appreciated and why?

Read Ruth 2 as an overview.

6. Look particularly at the interaction between Naomi and Ruth in Ruth 2:19-22.

This is an example of "rapport talk," which linguists say is typical between women. Rather than just reporting, as linguists say men often do, the women listen carefully, link on to what the other has said, and "take each other higher."

It begins, in verse 19a, by Naomi noticing Ruth's arms full of grain. What questions does she ask? How does this show she is "paying attention" to Ruth's life?

What are some specific ways a friend shows you she is "paying attention" to your life, to the things you say?

A. How does Ruth answer in verse 19b?

B. Boaz, as we will learn later, was a "kinsman-redeemer" who had a special responsibility to Naomi. How does Naomi respond to Ruth with enthusiasm and excitement in verse 20?

C. Naomi was excited, in part, because she sensed God was at work. In a Bible study group, women have opportunities to take one another higher when they sense God is at work. When someone has seen something in the Word or experienced a God moment in her life, how might you take her higher?

D. How does Ruth add to the excitement in 21? How could this happen in a Bible study group discussion?

E. How do you see Naomi's pleasure and conclusion in verse 22?

Think about women in your life who bless you by "paying attention" to your life, by drawing you out with questions, by being enthusiastic about God's work. Write down what women do conversationally that blesses you.

DAY 3
. . . .

Overcoming the Pain

Our depravity is deep, and our needs for attachment are strong. In Christ, we can respond to the pain our sin causes in a way that will overcome, break the chains, and unleash a gift that will not only bless us, but also the generations to come. I interviewed two women I deeply respect who overcame a conflict in their friendship through walking in repentance toward each other. Here is their story:

Kerry:

When Machelle and I met there was a connection right away. She had make-up on, and yet she homeschooled. I thought, "Wow—here is somebody who is fashionable and still homeschools." We had practically identical scores on The Meyers-Brigg personality test, our kids connected—but most of all, Machelle had such a passion for God. For five years we were blessed with a wonderful friendship. So when we fought that terrible day, it was devastating.

Machelle:

Friendship with Kerry is not something I've experienced with another woman—and so I really treasured what we had. That makes conflict all the more painful. It began, weirdly enough, about a peripheral doctrinal issue that I haven't even completely resolved in my own mind: infant baptism. Kerry and Bob visited our church, and I was so excited to think they might be coming to our church. Well—that was a very unusual day—one like I'd never seen—we had six infant baptisms.

Kerry:

Our friendship had gotten so easy—I was careless. When Machelle asked me what I thought, instead of thinking how she would feel, I just talked loosely, telling her some of the disparaging comments our kids made about infant baptism—things I shouldn't have repeated because they were disrespectful. I was uncaring in how I handled it.

Machelle:

My pride jumped up, and I got really defensive. Kerry could hear it. I could have closed my mouth and prayed about the right response—but I didn't.

Kerry:

The next day we had P.E. together for our kids, a homeschooling group, and Machelle came up to me, and I said, "Are we okay?" She nodded, but I could tell from the look in her eyes that we weren't. So we walked and talked and cried. People probably thought, Oh, those women.

Machelle:

We talked about infant baptism and agreed to disagree, and I don't even know if we disagree. But it wasn't even the issue of baptism—it was that we each reared our ugly heads. We were each sensitive enough to the Holy Spirit to admit we each had been wrong. We left P.E. okay—but not totally okay. Both a little edgy because we hadn't had conflict before. All afternoon I felt sick to my stomach.

That night I was in front of my computer—I started to call Kerry, and hung up thinking, She doesn't want to talk to me. I'm a rotten friend anyway. *Then I spent time praying and reading Scripture. After that, I knew the Lord's heart: "You've got to call her."*

So I did. I started crying right away. She'd obviously been weeping—and it was so encouraging to know that she had been weeping for me. She called herself an idiot, saying she'd been a terrible friend. We talked and cried for about two hours. I wouldn't want to live that day over, but it has really taken me to a different place in worshiping God. Kerry and I are kindred spirits, and we need each other to point each other to God.

Kerry and Machelle are two of the healthiest Christian women I know. Likewise, the Philippian church was a particularly healthy church, yet even within a healthy friendship, even within a healthy church, there will inevitably be pain and conflict. Why? Because we are sinners. Sooner or later we will reveal our feet of clay. Conflict between women is often excruciatingly painful because the friendships of women are typically closer than the friendships of men. It hurts a lot more to have a conflict with a soulmate than it does to have conflict with an acquaintance. In her book, *Just Friends*, Lillian Rubin wrote, "The pain of the demise of a soulmate friendship is akin to the pain of divorce."

7. What problem does Paul address in Philippians 4:2-3? What does he ask of the women? What does he ask of the church?

8. What evidence is there that Euodia and Syntyche were godly women? How is it that even people who truly love the Lord can cause conflict and pain?

9. What caused the conflict between Kerry and Machelle? Comment on how they resolved it and what you learned from them.

10. Describe our natural state according to Romans 3:9-18. Be specific.

11. How have you seen evidence of the above in your own life?

12. Read Philippians 2:1-11.

   A. According to verse 1, what are some of the joys of being united with Christ?

   B. On the basis of these joys, what appeal does Paul make in verse 2?

   C. What overcoming keys are given in verse 3? Think about a conflict in your life that was resolved or needs resolving. What impact did or could they keys have?

   D. What exhortation is given in verse 4? How might this overcome conflict?

E. In detail, describe the attitude of Jesus on the basis of verses 5-11.

F. In every conflict, you must begin with personal repentance. If you have a conflict in your life right now, ask yourself: How have I contributed to this problem? What could I repent of? What could I humbly confess with no excuses?

If your relationship with anyone is broken, strained, or even questionable, take the initiative to be reconciled. Assume that any fault is yours and be eager to confess it.
Dr. Greg Scharf, preaching professor at Trinity Evangelical Seminary

DAY 4

Three Generations, Three Models of Friendship

A hole in a cloth seems small until held up to the sun. As rays come streaming through, you realize how great the hole is. In the same way, the inadequacies of the best of our friendships as women may seem small—especially when compared to the friendships of men. Yet if we dare to hold our friendships up to the light of the scriptural models of friendship, we realize how far we have to go. As we study three generations of friendships in Scripture, a pattern will begin to emerge. Threads of strong and healthy spiritual friendships will appear and re-appear. When God repeats a refrain in Scripture we need to pay attention.

Beginning today, and continuing through next week's lessons, we will be examining "God's friendship pattern" as we juxtapose passages from three generations of these friends in Scripture:

- Ruth and Naomi
- David and Jonathan
- Mary and Elizabeth

While it is true that most women (and a few men—like David and Jonathan) have a gift for intimacy, that gift lays dormant in many of us—what can "quicken," it, bring it to life, is the Holy Spirit. Read carefully the following accounts and see if you can discover how an individual may have been receptive to the Holy Spirit's leading and acted upon it. Then describe how it impacted their friendship.

13. Read Ruth 1:15-17 and describe how God may have "quickened" Ruth and how she responded.

14. Read 1 Samuel 18:1-4 and describe how God may have "quickened" Jonathan and how he responded.

15. Read Luke 1:35-40 and describe how God "quickened" Mary and how she responded.

16. What common threads do you see running through the above passages? What does this say to you?

DAY 5

Reflections

One thread that winds its way through all three generations of friendship is godliness. These were individuals who loved God and desired to live reflective and "blameless" lives. Blameless in Scripture does not mean sinless, for we all sin every day in thought, word, or deed. What it means is that you walk in repentance—as soon as you are aware of sin, you confess and turn from it—and because God is faithful and just to forgive us our sins, and to cleanse us from all unrighteousness, we are blameless in His sight—the cleansing blood of Christ keeps us clean.

How does a believer become godly? It begins with a desire for godliness—to thirst as David did for the living God. David wrote:

> *As the deer pants for streams of water,*
> *So my soul pants for you, O God.*
> *My soul thirsts for God,*
> *for the living God.*
> Psalm 42:1-2

Ask the Lord to help you fall more deeply in love with Him, to thirst for Him, to pant for Him as the deer pants for water. Then run to the stream of living water, the Word of God. Our friendships will never be different from the friendships in the world unless we are filled, "quickened" with the Spirit of the Living God.

For this reason, woven throughout our study of friendships we shall also study Psalm 119, a psalm that tells how to be godly, how to be "quickened," or revived by the Spirit. This is the longest, and many believe, most wondrous psalm. It is made up of twenty-two octrains—twenty-two poems of eight verses each that flow through the Hebrew alphabet. Learning to meditate and then pray through Scripture is a key to godliness, and therefore, a key to profoundly impacting your friendships. Beginning next week, we will begin to pray through this psalm.

In reflection, today:

17. Write down what you will take away from this week's lesson.

18. If you are also reading the book, *The Friendships of Women,* what stood out to you from the first chapter?

19. What application will you make to your life?

PRAYER TIME

Learning to pray together can feel intimidating, but once you learn, you will find it to be one of the most gratifying experiences of Christian fellowship. This guide will gently lead you in this – so don't be afraid. You may be stretched a bit, but eventually you will rejoice. You may feel like the child who was afraid to swim and clung to the ladder, but one day, you did it! You didn't sink! And oh, how wonderful it feels to glide through the water! Just as there is support in the water, there is genuine support in praying together. He is there, He is not silent, and He listens to His children as they cry out together to Him.

A few common problems we will try to avoid:

* Too much talk—too little prayer. Sometimes women, because of their gift for intimacy and their ease with "rapport talk" can talk so long when they are explaining their prayer request, that there is no time to pray. For that reason, we need to learn to share our prayer request in prayer—and then allow others, who need to be paying close attention, to support us with sentence prayers.

* A lack of openness. Sometimes we hide behind praying for other people. Granted, it is wonderful to be an intercessor for others, but here, in this friendship circle, lift up your own needs and allow yourself to be supported by friends. Intercede for others on your own time, unless you are compelled by His Spirit to do otherwise. Ask here for yourself. Granted, it takes time to build trust, and you may not be ready to share that you struggle with a bad temper, money troubles, or sexual temptation. But you can begin by sharing things that Scripture says everyone needs—for example:

> Help me thirst for Your Word.
>
> Help me love You more.
>
> Give me wisdom in my relationships.

Openness is also facilitated by trust, so keep confidences!

- Praying outside of God's will. James says we have not because we ask not, and when we do ask, we ask "amiss." To help us ask within God's will, we will use Scripture, often, as our guideline.

Today—cluster in groups of four, at most, five. Each woman should choose one of the following prayers or a need she feels free to articulate.

- Lord, help me to better "pay attention" to the people You put in my life.
- Lord, help me to forgive as I have been forgiven.
- Lord, help me thirst for You more.
- Lord, help me love You more.
- Lord, help me understand Your Word.
- Lord, help me.......

After a woman has articulated her sentence prayer aloud, everyone should support her silently, and a few who are willing can support her audibly. Here is a model:

Sylvia: Lord, help me love You more.

Ann: I agree, Lord.

Dee: Yes, Lord, help Sylvia love You even more than she does.

Pause

Dee: Lord, help me to better "pay attention" to the people You put in my life.

Sylvia: I agree, Lord.

Pause

Now—cluster and follow the above pattern. Keep it short and simple. After you break the ice today, it will get easier and easier.

Two

Unleashing Our Gift

The July sun was finally sinking, promising relief from the heat. My husband, our daughter, and I sat motionless on the back porch, listening to the steady hum of cicadas, watching affectionately the antics of our six-month-old springer spaniel puppy. Unaffected by the heat, Effie enthusiastically chased a ball Sally tossed and carried it back proudly, tail wagging, eyes hopeful for a kind word or loving pat.

Reminiscing, I said, "When I was a little girl, I thought dogs were girls and cats were boys because dogs were so much friendlier."

To the great delight of her dad, eight-year-old Sally responded, "Mom, I'm sure you would say something like that with a guy right here!" We laughed at our daughter's protective reaction, especially because unknowingly Sally was proving my point. Studies show that females have greater sensitivity to the feelings of others. This is one of many ways that females tend to be friendlier than males. Women are much freer than men to be intimate with their own sex: Women will confide in each other, hug each other, and express their love for each other.

Long before there was DNA testing, cross-cultural studies or the ability to see the differences in the wiring of male and female brains—the Bible addressed our differences. "Male and female created he them" (Gen. 1:27 KJV). We are both created in the image of God, we are both, in Christ, of equal value, but we are, indeed, different. Most women seem to be gifted relationally.

Are women more intuitive? The evidence is strong, both scientifically and scripturally, that we are. But that intuitive gift can be used to hurt as well as to help. Little girls instinctively know how to go for the jugular—and often, they do! Are women more nurturing? Again, the evidence is strong that, generally speaking, we are. But our weakness is that sometimes we nurture when it would be more helpful to lovingly set boundaries or to speak the truth. Do women form stronger same-sex bonds? Again, the evidence is strong that we do. But that same gift can be abused, leading us into dependency upon people instead of upon God.

In our depravity we have abused God's good gifts. Both sex and food are good gifts from God, but man has abused them, often causing these gifts to bring harm instead of a blessing. As women, God has given us a gift for intimacy. But again, we have often abused our gift. How can we avoid this and instead unleash our gift for great good?

It begins with being a worshiper of God, and we'll consider that today. Then, we must follow the instructions of our Maker. His Word is a light unto our feet and can penetrate our natural darkness. This week we will introduce a few of the threads that appear and reappear in the models of friendship God has given us in His Word. We will also begin to pray through Psalm 119, for it is vital that we pray God's Word. The two most powerful weapons we have against the enemy are prayer and His Word. Using them together should be a habit of our lives.

Psalm 119 is the longest psalm and the psalm that exalts God's Word. Dietrich Bonhoeffer, the young man who took a courageous stand against Hitler and was martyred for his faith, wrote in his book, *Psalms: The Prayer Book of the Bible:*

> *It is a dangerous error, surely very widespread among Christians, to think that the heart can pray by itself. . . . Prayer does not mean simply to pour out one's heart. It means rather to find the way to God and to speak with him, whether the heart is full or empty. No man can do that by himself. For that he needs Jesus Christ.*

> *. . . If we wish to pray with confidence and gladness, then the Words of Holy Scripture will have to be the solid basis of our prayer. For here we know that Jesus Christ, the Word of God, teaches us to pray.*

Sometimes Christians, in a reaction against memorized formal prayers that may have become dead when parroted, want to only pray spontaneously. John Piper has said that good prayer needs to be both free and formed. If you are only praying memorized formal prayers, your prayers can become dead. If you are only praying spontaneously, your prayers can become shallow and trite. One of the reasons I encourage praying through the Psalms is so that our prayers will be rich and true. You will also find that by praying "formed" prayers, your free prayers will begin to grow in depth.

Four out of five days each week you will open or close your time with God in prayer, taking either half or a whole octrain (eight verses) from Psalm 119. Sometimes you can pray the passage verbatim and it works! Sometimes it won't because the situation the psalmist is facing is very different than your own, yet you can still take the situation the psalmist is in and find an application to your life. For example, you may not be being chased by a physical army, but we always have a spiritual battle against enemies in high places, and so we can make the psalm our own. Today, it would be appropriate to pray responsively —in other words, read a verse, and then make it your own. For example, with Psalm 119:1-4, read each verse aloud, and then follow it with a prayer similar to what I have done:

Blessed are they whose ways are blameless,
who walk according to the law of the LORD.

> May I walk blamelessly today, LORD, walking according to Your Word.

Blessed are they who keep his statutes
and seek him with all their heart.

> May I keep Your statutes. May I seek You with all my heart.

They do nothing wrong;
they walk in his ways.

> May I do nothing wrong. May I walk in Your ways.

You have laid down precepts
that are to be fully obeyed.

> May I remember Your Word and fully obey.

DAY 1

Worshipers

As sweet as the sisterhood of women is, it pales in comparison to the power, perspective, and love we can have as sisters in Christ. How God has strengthened me with "sisters" who were so filled with Him that their heart overflow spilled out to me. What these women had in common was not just that they knew the Lord, but that they were worshipers of God.

We will begin today by looking at a woman who absolutely had a gift for intimacy—she had so many of the qualities that scientists are now discovering are typical of women. She was intuitive, she was nurturing, and she was unafraid of intimacy. But what unleashed her gift and caused her to go down in history was that she was a worshiper of God. It is one thing to worship well, it is quite another to be a worshiper of God. True worship always involves honor, and we honor God by giving our whole selves to Him in adoration, obedience, and sacrifice. Mary of Bethany was a worshiper of God. Mary loved Jesus with her whole heart, and that is evident every time we meet her. The first time we meet her is in Luke 10. Meditate on the following description of her:

She had a sister, Mary, who sat before the Master, hanging on every word he said.

Luke 10:39 *(MSG)*

1. Describe Mary of Bethany from the above verse.

Now, before you dive into today's study, prepare your heart by praying through the very first four verses of Psalm 119. Like Mary of Bethany, thirst for God; pray through it, asking Him to cause it to live in your life.

Blessed are they whose ways are blameless,
who walk according to the law of the LORD.

Blessed are they who keep his statutes
and seek him with all their heart.

They do nothing wrong;
they walk in his ways.

You have laid down precepts
that are to be fully obeyed.

Psalm 119:1-4

As background for today's amazing scene, it is important to know that Mary of Bethany is the sister of Martha and Lazarus. When Mary was sitting at Jesus' feet, hanging on His every word, Martha was angry. She came to Jesus and asked Him to rebuke Mary for not helping her in the kitchen. Jesus told Martha that Mary had chosen the most important thing, and it would not be taken away from her. What is the most important thing? To love the Lord with all our heart, soul, and mind. This describes a worshiper. A worshiper gives honor to Jesus with her teachable heart, devotion, obedience, and sacrifice. (Service can be worship as well, when it is about honoring Jesus, but Jesus sees the hearts of both sisters here, and Martha's heart was not right.) How I love this story, for it shows that Jesus was protecting a woman, valuing her every bit as much as a man, wanting her to learn and to sit at His feet. This happened in the beginning of Jesus' ministry.

Years later, at the end of Jesus' ministry on earth, Lazarus becomes very ill, and the sisters send word to Jesus. But Jesus purposely does not rush to his bedside. Lazarus dies.

Mary is devastated. When Jesus finally arrives, four days after the burial of her brother, she falls at His feet, weeping, saying, "Lord, if you had been here, my brother would not have died" (John 11:32). Jesus weeps with her, for we are told He loved her. Then, Jesus astonishes everyone by bringing Lazarus back from the dead.

In the scene we will study today, a party is being thrown in celebration of the raising of Lazarus. Mary enters carrying her alabaster bottle. In the days of Jesus, women who reached marriage age were given, by their parents, an alabaster bottle or box filled with precious perfume. This was their most precious possession, their dowry, and when they were betrothed, they would break it at the feet of their intended, symbolizing their willingness to sacrifice their most precious possession for their beloved.

WARMUP

Ask what differences they have noticed between the friendships of women and the friendships of men.

2. Read John 12:1-7 as an overview.

   A. Read John 12:1-2 and be a detective. In narrative sections, ask the journalistic questions of who, what, why, when, and how. Take time here.

   B. Where was this party happening? How far (look at a Bible map) was this from Jerusalem, where Jesus would die? Significance?

   C. Why was this party happening?

   D. Who were the guests?

   E. When did this happen? Significance?

   F. How do you think the various participants were feeling?

3. Describe everything you see from John 12:3. Make at least five observations from the verse and another five from the context (surrounding verses).

Austin Stone, a large church in Austin, Texas, made up of mostly twenty-somethings, has a young pastor named Matt Carter. While preaching on this passage (11/5/05) he described how intimate Mary was. He gave this illustration:

My wife Jennifer is seated in the front row. I don't mind if a man from this congregation has an animated conversation with her, pats her on the shoulder, or even gives her a hug, as long as it's a side hug. But if he starts stroking her hair, I'm going to go Old Testament on him!

A woman's hair is intimate. Also, Jewish women didn't unbind their hair in public. For Mary to loosen her long hair from her tight bun, and in public, was astonishing. She is motivated by the love pouring out of her heart for Jesus—she loved Him for who He was, how He had treated her as a woman, and what He had done for her family. She had to get her most precious possession and pour it on the feet of Jesus. Then, without even thinking, she quickly unbinds her hair to wipe His precious fragrance-soaked feet. Think about how this ministered to Jesus —in just six days He will be crucified. But her precious perfume was surely still lingering on His body, letting Him know, that in the midst of hate and betrayal, there was one who loved Him. What an amazing demonstration of a woman's gift for intimacy!

4. Why do you think Mary did this? How did it impact Mary, Jesus, and the others?

Read Mark 14:3-9

5. In Mark 14:6-9, find eight to ten ways that Jesus praises or defends Mary.

6. What do you think it means to be a worshiper of God? Do you think you are a worshiper? Explain.

DAY 2
....

God's Friendship Pattern

This amazing story of Mary anointing Jesus shows so many threads from God's friendship pattern. Mary of Bethany was definitely a **risk taker**, for what she is about to do is amazing. This was **a parting scene**, for she knew, we are told later by Jesus, that He was about to die. She was encouraging, sacrificing, and showing **unfailing love**. The reason, however, that she lived out all these threads from God's friendship pattern was because she was a **worshiper**. Without this, her gift for intimacy would never have been unleashed the way it was. Part of being a worshiper is to pray through Scripture with your whole heart. Finish yesterday's octrain by praying again responsively, asking Him to help you keep His Word and to bless you as you do.

Oh, that my ways were steadfast
in obeying your decrees!

Then I would not be put to shame
when I consider all your commands.

> *I will praise you with an upright heart*
> *as I learn your righteous laws.*
>
> *I will obey your decrees;*
> *do not utterly forsake me.*
>
> **Psalm 119:5-8**

Mary of Bethany exemplified so many of the threads we will be studying, in depth, in this guide. As an overview, meditate on the following passages and consider how she provides a model for the particular thread mentioned.

7. Mary of Bethany and God's Friendship Pattern

    A. **Worshiper of God—Luke 10:39 (or other verses you see)**

    B. **Vulnerability—John 11:28-33**

    C. **Risk Taker—Mark 14:3-5**

    D. **Unfailing Love—Mark 14:8a ("a" designates the first part of the verse)**

    E. **Parting Scene—Mark 14:8b**

An important thread to consider, early on, is that of being a risk taker, as Mary of Bethany was. I have learned, both from Scripture and from life, that taking risks is essential if friendships are going to be deep.

Friendship cannot begin without at least one person taking a risk of reaching out. Friendship cannot progress beyond the surface unless there is honest and vulnerable sharing from the heart.

Friendship can occur within a small group, but some groups progress better than others. One of the ways the soil can be prepared for friendship seeds that will sprout and blossom to lasting fruit is to pray and determine that you as an individual, and the group as a whole, will be trustworthy. When someone shares from the heart, you must keep her confidence within the group. If someone shares something shocking, you must determine to give grace, to think the best, and to pray for her. She is trusting you!

8. What are some of qualities in a group that would make you willing to be open, vulnerable, and honest?

DAY 3

Greeting Scenes

God seems to zoom His camera in when two people, who will be significant in one another's lives, meet. As you see this pattern, you will realize that when someone comes across your path for the first time, you must be alert, for God may be in it! This sensitivity to the Spirit of God may help you seize God-ordained friendships that you might have otherwise missed.

Today you will see how Mary recognized that God was giving her an understanding friend in Elizabeth, so she hurried to go see Elizabeth. Likewise, it's fascinating to see how quickly Jonathan bonded to David in their greeting scene. God knew what trials the future held for David, so He provided the perfect supportive friend for David.

You may look around your small-group Bible study and wonder if you will become close to any of the women. I have learned that we need to be open and sensitive to God's leading. One newlywed woman told me, "When I first met Ginny, I never thought we would be friends—because Ginny was so old." (Ginny was thirty-two.) "But oh, how she has modeled for me how to love Jesus and to walk with Him. I'm so thankful she persisted in friendship with me." When we were children, we chose friends on the basis of age, appearance, and popularity. It is time to put childish ways aside and choose instead, on the basis of the leading of God's Word and God's Spirit.

9. State the principle given in each of the following verses that can guide you in choosing close friends.

   A. Proverbs 13:20

   B. 1 Corinthians 15:33

10. In all three of our friendship models, we see that someone may have been drawn to an individual in friendship because she was impressed with that individual's walk with the Lord. She discovered a "worshiper" and was drawn. Write down everything you discover about the individual from the following passages.

   A. What did Boaz know about Ruth according to Ruth 2:11?

B. David was Ruth's great grandson, and his story follows the book of Ruth in Samuel. When Jonathan met David, David was still holding the head of Goliath. Describe, according to 1 Samuel 17:33-37, what King Saul's son, Jonathan, knew about David.

C. Mary was a descendant of David and also Elizabeth's relative. What was Elizabeth's reputation according to Luke 1:5-7?

11. How important is godliness to you in choosing your closest friends?

12. In the following greeting scenes, God zooms His camera in. We therefore, should be attentive to detail. Write down everything you observe.

A. 1 Samuel 18:1-4

It is important to realize that Jonathan, as the son of King Saul, was next in line to be king. His actions, therefore, are terribly significant. He is taking off his "kingly" garments and placing them on David. As we will continue to study these two friends, you will see how important Jonathan was in David's life. Jonathan was obviously God's provision to David for protection and encouragement.

B. Luke 1:34-45

13. Can you remember a time when you sensed God was giving you the gift of a friend? What do you remember about your "greeting scene" that made you think God might have been involved?

Pray responsively through the following passage:

How can a young man keep his way pure?
By living according to your word.

I seek you with all my heart;
do not let me stray from your commands.

I have hidden your word in my heart
that I might not sin against you.

Praise be to you, O Lord;
teach me your decrees.

Psalm 119:9-12

DAY 4

. . . .

Parting Scenes

When I am a detached observer of parting scenes and greeting scenes in airports, I experience a quiet joy. Lovers lingering in bittersweet embraces. Grandparents ecstatic over the first sight of a newborn grandchild. Sisters hugging in reunion with unabashed tears. As I watch from the safety of my waiting-room chair, my heart is warmed.

It is much more exhausting to be an active participant. For it's in these most poignant of moments that latent emotion in a friendship boils to the surface. If we truly have bonded with a friend, then it is a tearing apart. It hurts. But it can also be amazingly sweet. As Romeo said to Juliet, "Parting is such sweet sorrow." There is a bittersweet satisfaction in realizing that it wouldn't hurt so much if we didn't care so much.

When I wrote the original edition of *The Friendships of Women,* my husband and I were young with three children. But twenty more years brought two more daughters, a daughter-in-law, a son-in-law, and four grandchildren. In 2004, my precious fifty-nine-year-old husband, Steve, went to be with the Lord, losing his valiant fight with colon cancer. When Steve was dying, he called each of our five children and our precious daughter-in-law to his bed to say good-bye. Steve knew how important "parting scenes" were, saying what each will always remember. Annie, our youngest, shared:

> *I crawled up on his bed and he just held me for a long time. We could just be silent together—I loved that. … He just kept holding me, and he was crying. "Annie, I'm so sorry I have to leave you. I'm so sorry. I'm so glad I got to be your daddy. Annie, I will always be your daddy. Always. I will always be your daddy."*

Those words are etched in Annie's memory forever, giving comfort. As painful as it was, as painful as it is for me to read them, I am so very glad he said them. Though parting may be hard and sorrow may be deep, it is not wasted sadness. Your presence may give comfort. Closing expressions of love may give consolation for years to come. The more final the good-bye, the greater the bleeding, but the more cherished the memory.

Steve learned the importance of parting scenes from the pattern of Scripture. Two of the most poignant passages in all of Scripture are the parting scenes in Ruth and 1 Samuel. Since these models have helped me to realize the value of partings, as I hope they will for you, my attitude toward these painful moments has changed. In the last four years I have been at the deathbeds of my husband, my father, and my mother. I was able to tell each of them of my love before their souls fled. I am so thankful I didn't shrink from the pain but seized each of those parting scenes. Though we live in a world of mobility, and friends may only be in our lives for a season, I will still throw myself into friendship. How sad if we deprive ourselves of friendship because of the pain of saying good-bye. Parting is hard, but it is a sweet sorrow, and we see that so clearly in the passages we will study today.

First, we will consider the parting scene between Naomi and her daughters-in-law. Naomi has sometimes been called a "female Job" because she suffered so many losses. In the following scene, Naomi is leaving the land of Moab where her husband and sons died. When she discovers her daughters-in-law want to come with her to Bethlehem, she encourages them instead to go back to Moab where they will have a better chance of remarrying.

14. Read Ruth 1:8-17

    A. In verses 8-9, write down all the ways Naomi affirmed and blessed her daughters-in-law in this parting scene.

    B. In verses 9-10, find all the ways her daughters-in-law expressed their love for her.

    C. In verses 11-13, list the reasons that Naomi has lost hope. What reasons does she give for sending the girls back? What other reasons might there be?

    D. In verse 14, how do the girls again show their love for Naomi?

    E. In the famous passage of 15-17, Ruth chooses not to part. What evidence do you find in this passage for her love for Naomi? What sacrifices may she be making?

Each time my husband and I moved to a new state, there have been tearful parting scenes between my sisters in Christ and myself. And though we as women pride ourselves on being able to express our love, there were several times when I truly didn't realize how much my friends cared until the parting. When we were loading the moving van in Akron, Steve called up the stairs, "Dee, you have a visitor!" I was surprised to find Phyllis, a woman from my Bible study, perched quietly on a big box in the living room.

Phyllis had never been to see me before. My surprise grew as she silently held out a beautiful afghan. For months she had been spending evenings crocheting this expression of love. Phyllis, undisputedly the most reserved member of all the women in the study, loved me! Spontaneously, I hugged her. At first her arms hung limply at her sides, but then she returned my embrace. Tears ran unchecked down our cheeks.

When King Saul was trying to kill David, Saul's son, Jonathan, couldn't believe his father would be so evil. David tries to convince Jonathan of his need for protection. Finally, Jonathan listens with a teachable heart and agrees to a test that will reveal his father's motives. Saul flunks the test, and Jonathan then helps David to flee to safety. Before David goes, there is perhaps the most poignant parting scene in all of Scripture.

15. Read 1 Samuel 20:32-42.

  A. In verses 32-34, why was Jonathan grieved?

  B. Describe the emotion in verse 41. Write down everything you discover. Why do you think there was so much pain?

  C. What do you think Shakespeare meant when he said: "Parting is such sweet sorrow"? How do you see this in the above parting scenes?

  D. How does Jonathan help David in verse 42? Write down everything you discover.

Kathleen tells of having a good cry with her best friend when Kathleen was about to move across the country.

I sobbed, "What will I do without you?"

She said, "You'll be fine."

I wanted to say, "How can you say that? I won't be fine! I'll be miserable!" But that was truly the best thing she could have said to me. If she had allowed herself to continue to be as morose and depressed as I was, then she couldn't have helped me. Instead she gave me strength. She was really truly being my friend.

16. Can you remember a "parting scene" that has ministered to you personally as the years have gone by? Share something about it.

17. Often, God doesn't permit us the knowledge that we are parting from someone. Are there those in your life to whom you need to express your love in case that happens? How might you seize some moments in the near future?

Even small partings can bring small comforts. I treasure those golden moments as a mother when I tucked a cuddly toddler under her favorite blanket with one last bear hug. Her sweet smile, her arm-spread "I love you this much!" linger in my memory as her childhood fades away. And I have learned the most meaningful moments of a friend's visit may occur when I take the trouble to walk her to her car. The very act of showing that I care enough to prolong the visit often releases from her a confidence or expression of love that we both treasure. If I'm not willing to create these parting scenes, then they slip between the cracks of time, never to be called to remembrance when remembrance is sorely needed.

18. How might you better seize "small partings?"

DAY 5

Reflections

Pray responsively through the rest of this octrain, asking God to help you delight in His Word as the psalmist does.

With my lips I recount
all the laws that come from your mouth.

I rejoice in following your statutes
as one rejoices in great riches.

I meditate on your precepts
and consider your ways.

I delight in your decrees;
I will not neglect your word.

Psalm 119:13-16

19. The psalmist has said he will "recount all the laws that come from God's mouth." See if you can remember five of the friendship threads we have considered in the study so far. After each one, give a scriptural example and then a way you might apply it to your life.

A. Thread? Example? Application?

B. Thread? Example? Application?

C. Thread? Example? Application?

D. Thread? Example? Application?

E. Thread? Example? Application?

20. If you are also reading from the book, *The Friendships of Women,* what stood out to you from chapter 2?

21. Has this week's study impressed anything particular on you that could lead to a personal prayer request? Write down a sentence concerning that, or concerning another personal need, that you would be willing to lift up in prayer.

PRAYER TIME

Cluster in groups of three or four. Have each woman lift up her answer to question 21 in prayer, and then allow the others to support her. When there is a pause, another woman should lift up her need.

Three

The Darker Side of Being Crazy-Glued

Our gift for intimacy, as women, and particularly, as sisters in Christ, can be beautiful. If our relationship with the Lord is strong, then sweet water overflows, and the fluidity in our relationships means we can have a lovely effect on each other. Like gently moving streams joining into one river, we round the difficult bends of life together, strengthening one another with a fresh water supply. We are free, flowing, and unconcerned with boundaries. This is part of the beauty of the friendships of women, but it is also the danger.

We are afraid to run toward the ocean alone. We feel a sense of panic in solitude. Ironically, it is because we place such a high value on our relationships that we are tempted, sometimes, to be so very cruel. It is most evident in childhood.

How I remember Tricia, the little girl who lived next door and looked like Pippi Longstocking, with freckles, red braids, and an infectious grin. Tricia loved it when I told Bible stories. She responded to Christ in true repentance when she was only six. She honored me with her trust and often came to me with her joys and sorrows. One day I was getting my newspaper when Tricia came running up to me, braids bouncing, bursting to tell me:

Mrs. Brestin—guess what!

What, Tricia?

I have a new friend! Her name is Jill. She's so nice. She asked me to sit with her at lunch yesterday, and today I saved her a seat! We walked part way home together, and I might get to go to her house for an overnight on Friday!

I smiled, remembering those days when having a best friend was bliss and not having one was misery.

The very next day Tricia appeared at my door with red eyes, slumped shoulders, and a quivering mouth. She handed me a wadded up note, explaining haltingly: "Jill's best friend taped this to my locker."

We sat down together on the porch step. I put one arm around Tricia and with the other un-crumpled the offending note, spreading it out on my lap. When I read it through, despite my compassion for my wounded little neighbor, I had to suppress a smile, not only at the humor in the note, but at the delight I felt in having captured a perfect specimen of the treachery of girls.

> Dear Tricia,
> Stay away from Jill. Jill is my best friend and you are trespassing.
>
> Don't save Jill a seat at lunch.
> Don't wait for her at her locker.
> Don't give her notes in the hall.
>
> Is this clear?
> Jill is my best friend and you must find a different best friend.
> Stay away!!!
>
> Love, Kelly

Do we change when we become women? We may only become more subtle. I will share with you how I had some of the same feelings as Kelly did, when my closest friend was getting another friend—except, instead of being a third-grader, I was in my thirties.

This week we will consider our root problem, and why it manifests itself as it does more strongly in women. We will learn how this can, indeed, be overcome in Christ. We must also learn, as mothers and as mentors, how to help the next generation of girls. Cruelty has escalated in this generation, and it is a fortunate girl who has someone who can help her navigate through the crocodile-infested swamps of junior high and high school.

Plan a date to get together and "break bread" (soup and bread, pizza, potato bar...) in the next few weeks. It will be a time when you will affirm one another. your facilitator should e-mail everyone to confirm when, where, and what! (Instructions for blessing time in Leader's Helps.)

DAY 1

Created to Worship

Before beginning your study, pray through this passage, asking God to open your eyes. This is a prayer you can actually pray verbatim. If the last verse isn't true of you, ask Him to make it true!

Do good to your servant, and I will live;
I will obey your word.

Open my eyes that I may see
wonderful things in your law.

I am a stranger on earth;
do not hide your commands from me.

My soul is consumed with longing
for your laws at all times.

Psalm 119:17-20

WARMUP

Have you noticed territorial tendencies in little girls, or do you remember or see them now in yourself? If so, share an observation or brief memory.

God created us with a yearning to worship. Pascal said that each of us has a "God-shaped vacuum." The key verse in the book of Ecclesiastes puts it like this:

> *He has made everything beautiful in its time. He has also set eternity in the hearts of men; yet they cannot fathom what God has done from beginning to end.*

> Ecclesiastes 3:11

1. What two statements are made about God in the above verse? What one statement is made about man?

Because man has "eternity in his heart," but also cannot fathom what God has done, his worship is often misdirected. He makes a false god—in the Old Testament days, and even today, people worshiped gods of stone, gods they had made with their own hands.

2. In Psalm 115:

A. This psalm was sung at Passover, a time when God's people remembered His mighty works on their behalf to deliver them from Egyptian slavery. How does the psalm begin (verse 1)? Where do the believers want praise directed?

B. What acts might they be remembering? (Ps. 78:12-16 recounts some of those acts.)

C. It is often true that, on this earth, unbelievers may live in ease while true believers may suffer. What taunt is given from the heathen in verse 2?

When I am suffering on this earth, I hold on to the truth of Ecclesiastes 3:11—"He makes everything beautiful in His time." We cannot even imagine the glory that awaits us or the recompense for those who suffered trusting God. It truly will be okay in the end, and if it isn't okay, then it isn't the end yet.

What affirmation is made in verse 3 about God's power? For those believers who knew He was good, how might this be a comfort in suffering?

D. List everything expressed about the idols in verses 4-7.

E. What startling statement is made in verse 8? What do you think this means?

DAY 2

Worshiping Things "Under the Sun"

Often man, instead of worshiping gods of silver, gold, or stone, will worship other things "under the sun." These are gods of money, sex, food, power, and people—to name a few. These false gods are worshiped not only by the heathen, but also by God's people. It's easier to see that worshiping stone gods is wrong than it is to see that it is wrong to make anything or anyone "under the sun" the object of our trust.

The book of Ecclesiastes is written by Solomon. (Some commentators believe it was a man posing as Solomon, to make a point—but in any case, the meaning is the same. There is no strong evidence to dispute Solomon's authorship.) When Solomon was young and had just become king, and God told him He would give Solomon whatever his heart desired, Solomon asked for wisdom. God was so pleased with this that He not only gave Solomon great wisdom and discernment, but also two gifts Solomon had not asked for:

"riches and honor" (1 Kings 3:13). Solomon walked with the Lord in these early years, and the Lord actually appeared to him twice.

But as time passed, something happened to Solomon's walk with the Lord, and he began to disregard the very wisdom he had been given, lost fervor for the Lord, and then felt the emptiness we can all feel, whether we are an unbeliever or a believer, when we turn from our love relationship with God. Later, when God sums up Solomon's life, He says that Solomon failed to continue in Him, and failed to love Him as his father David had loved Him. As you pray through the following section in Psalm 119, you can see what the attitude of a king should be. Pray for your country's leader and pray for yourself as well.

You rebuke the arrogant, who are cursed
and who stray from your commands.

Remove from me scorn and contempt,
for I keep your statutes.

Though rulers sit together and slander me,
your servant will meditate on your decrees.

Your statutes are my delight;
they are my counselors.
Psalm 119:21-24

3. Read 1 Kings 11:1-6.

    A. What warning and command had God given all the Israelites, according to verse 2?

    B. Perhaps as king, Solomon felt "above" that command. Every single one of us is good at deceiving ourselves when we want to sin. Describe what Solomon did, according to verses 1-5.

    C. How is Solomon's life summarized in verse 6?

When our love relationship with God is not vibrant, we still have that God-shaped void, and we long to fill it—so we, as Solomon did, go looking for love in all the wrong places. It can look the same for men and women—for both genders are tempted by some of the same things, and both genders can try to anesthetize their pain in some of the same dead-end ways. But it can also look different, for studies show that the primary drive for women is connection; whereas, the primary drive for men is status. It is interesting to read Ecclesiastes and to see some of the misdirected ways that Solomon, as a man, tried to fill his God-shaped void.

4. Read Ecclesiastes 1:12-18.

   A. What are some of the ways Solomon describes himself and his position of status in this passage?

   B. What sorrowful conclusions does he come to in verses 13 and 18?

This life is difficult—both because of man's sin and because of the judgment of God. Every single one of us experiences the pain of life. Our choice is to humble ourselves under the mighty hand of the one true God or to turn to other gods.

5. Describe some of the places Solomon turns in:
   A. Ecclesiastes 2:1-3

   B. Ecclesiastes 2:4-8

6. Read Ecclesiastes 2:9-11

   A. How does Solomon describe his status in verse 9?

   B. Because of his wealth and power, Solomon does us the favor of testing many of the things that people think will fill up that void, that "eternity" in their hearts. What was Solomon able to do according to verse 10?

   C. If you had the power to give yourself anything, what do you think your life would look like?

   D. Does Solomon find any delight in this? (v. 10)

E. What is his conclusion? (v. 11) Why, do you think?

The word *vanity* means "something passing swiftly away." It may be translated "fleeting," "passing," or "meaningless." It permeates Ecclesiastes. Ecclesiastes often seems very "male," but we as women can be tempted to run after the wrong things too. We don't want to become the most powerful ruler or to collect a harem, but we have our own ways of trying to gain the praise of others. Often we are driven to be beautiful, hoping that will make us admired and loved. Pick up any secular women's magazine and notice how most of it is dedicated to our outward appearance.

7. How is the word *vanity* (or some translations say "fleeting" or "passing") used in Proverbs 31:30? Have you experienced this?

8. New Testament authors also address this drive in women. What is taught in 1 Peter 3:3-4?

DAY 3

The Terror for Women

Psychiatrist Jean Baker Miller of Wellesley College's Stone Center explains that the terror for women is isolation. Their sense of worth is grounded in the ability to make and maintain relationships. When men attempt suicide, it is often because of a loss of status: a lost income, a lost job, or a lost reputation. When women attempt suicide, it is usually because of failures involving lovers, family, or friends.

What this reveals is that we, as the relational sex, tend to worship people instead of the one true God. Just as it was vanity for Solomon to put his trust in wealth or position, it is vanity for us to put our trust in people. As dear as our loved ones may be, they will not and/or cannot always be there for us. They may betray us, move away, or die. I was blessed with an amazing husband, and he tried with his whole heart not to die, but he died young. God has gently pried my fingers away from clinging too tightly to people—a pattern I have demonstrated all my life—with friends, with children, and with my husband. In my pain, God has comforted me and helped me to turn more fully to Him as my source of love, wisdom, and strength. I identify more strongly with Naomi now, who also was widowed young, but who, in time, found God faithful. In this first year of widowhood

I am clinging to the promises in His Word. Today's passage is a meaningful one to pray through when you are hurting. If you are not hurting now, you can pray for someone who is.

I am laid low in the dust;
preserve my life according to your word.

I recounted my ways and you answered me;
teach me your decrees.

Let me understand the teaching of your precepts;
then I will meditate on your wonders.

My soul is weary with sorrow;
strengthen me according to your word.

Psalm 119:25-28

I am recounting the promises of God, that I will see Steve again and that he is experiencing fullness of joy. I hold on to God's promise to be a husband to the widow and a father to the fatherless. God is strengthening me with His Word and His Spirit as I meditate on His precepts.

I still cherish my friends and my children, and I look forward to being re-united with Steve one golden day, but I know I must hold each precious person loosely and not see him or her as my source of security. People cannot be what only God can be, and they will, unlike God, let me down, for they have a sin nature. If I am shocked when they do let me down, it is because I have made them into gods, not recognizing their feet of clay.

God tells us not to trust in people, not because He is unkind, but because He cares so deeply for us. He wants the best for us, and therefore, He exhorts us to put our roots down deeply into Him, and Him alone.

9. Read Jeremiah 17:5-10 thoughtfully, a passage that is very similar to Psalm 1. Poetry in the Scripture often uses parallelism, which is a helpful interpretive tool. If you don't understand one line, then the next thought, if it is a parallel thought, will give light to the preceding thought.

   A. What does the Lord say in verse 5? What two things does this person do that are destructive?

   B. Find all the descriptions you can of this person from verse 6.

C. What parallel characteristics are given about the person who is blessed?

D. How is this person described in verse 8? Find at least six parts of the description.

E. What truth do we learn about ourselves according to verse 9?

F. What are some ways that you have been deceived by your own heart? Consider times you have made more choices or succumbed to temptation.

G. Who does understand us, according to verse 10? What should this teach us?

10. Read this passage again in the *Amplified Bible*, underlining phrases that help you understand what God is saying. Write down any new observations after each verse.

Thus says the Lord: Cursed [with great evil] is the strong man who trusts in and relies on frail man, making weak [human] flesh his arm, and whose mind and heart turn aside from the Lord.

For he shall be like a shrub or a person naked and destitute in the desert; and he shall not see any good come, but shall dwell in the parched places in the wilderness, in an uninhabited salt land.

[Most] blessed is the man who believes in, trusts in, and relies on the Lord, and whose hope and confidence the Lord is.

For he shall be like a tree planted by the waters that spreads out its roots by the river; and it shall not see and fear when heat comes; but its leaf shall be green. It shall not be anxious and full of care in the year of drought, nor shall it cease yielding fruit.

The heart is deceitful above all things, and it is exceedingly perverse and corrupt and severely, mortally sick! Who can know it [perceive, understand, be acquainted with his own heart and mind]?

I the Lord search the mind, I try the heart, even to give to every man according to his ways, according to the fruit of his doings.

11. How would you apply today's lesson?

DAY 4

Overcoming Territorial Tendencies

When I was in my early thirties, Steve and I moved from Seattle to Fargo, North Dakota. Moving is harder for women than for men because we are so relational. I started praying months before the move for a kindred spirit in Fargo.

We'd been in Fargo for just a few months when I met Ann through a church we'd visited. I was drawn to her and invited her for coffee. When I asked her how she had come to Christ, she told me about the deep hunger she had for spiritual truth as a college student, and how she felt like "The Hollow Men" in TS Eliot's poem. I, too, had been moved by TS Eliot's poetry in college, and I immediately sensed a "kindred spirit" as Anne of Green Gables was so fond of saying. Ann and I were soon finishing one another's sentences.

Just months later, Ann told me, with great excitement, "My very best friend in all the world is moving to Fargo!" Though I smiled on the outside, I was sure that my friendship with Ann, which had sprung up so quickly, was in danger of being crowded out in its infancy before it had a chance to grow strong and tall. Ann raved about Sylvia and her husband, Kendall, who was coming to work with Ann's husband. Kendall and Howie had been close since their days together at Trinity Seminary. Not only were Sylvia and Ann soul mates, their husbands were as well! I felt the cold wind approaching: Sylvia and Ann would be as snug as bugs in a rug—and I would be outside, shivering in the bitter Fargo winter!

But that isn't what happened. Ann also raved to Sylvia about me and arranged for the three of us to have lunch together. Sylvia didn't seem threatened by me in the least, just terribly eager to meet me. Our time together that day was one of the most special fellowships in my memory. Sparks went from one to another as we sharpened one another with our understanding of Scripture and of thoughts from various Christian authors. Laughter abounded. Afterward we walked and prayed together—experiencing the joy of a three-fold cord.

Nearly twenty-five years later, Ann and Sylvia are still dear to me. Though we are "long-distance" friends for the most part, e-mail and cell phones have shortened that distance, and we continue to help one another find strength in God.

Why did our "threesome" survive? I believe it is because Ann and Sylvia, like Mary of Bethany, are worshipers of God. They allowed a third person into their friendship circle because their deepest needs were being met by the one true God—so they were open and welcoming to a third friend, rather than exclusive and guarded, as little girls are.

It is always true, when we long to be released from the bondage of idolatry, whether that idol is money, food, or a person—that it isn't enough to stop worshiping a false god, we must start worshiping the one true God, allowing Him to meet our deepest needs. The following passage from Psalm 119 shows the joy of being set free from the deceit of idolatry. Pray responsively through it before you begin your study.

Keep me from deceitful ways;
be gracious to me through your law.

I have chosen the way of truth;
I have set my heart on your laws.

I hold fast to your statutes, O LORD;
do not let me be put to shame.

I run in the path of your commands,
for you have set my heart free.

Psalm 119:29-32

12. Comment on Dee's story with her friends Ann and Sylvia. What was the main point?

In each of our three models, we find friends who were also worshipers of God, so they were set free of worshiping people. They cherished their friends and family, but they did not cling to them in an unhealthy way. Perhaps the one who particularly stands out as a worshiper of God is David, about whom God Himself said "is a man after my heart." The friendship of David and Jonathan is beautiful, and it is even said that their souls were knit together, but instead of helping each other find strength in each other, they helped each other find strength in God, the true object of their worship.

Read Psalm 5.

13. With what three requests does David open this psalm to His Lord and His King?

14. Describe the picture you see of David from verse 3.

15. Verse 9 is quoted in Romans 3, the famous passage where the whole world is declared guilty before God. What does David realize about man?

16. How does understanding the sinfulness of man, help one to:

    A. Not worship man

    B. Not be surprised when our dearest friends and family let us down

17. Who should be our ultimate source of joy, and why, according to verses 11-12?

Read Psalm 63.

18. What phrases in verse 1 demonstrate David's longing for God?

19. How has God proven Himself to be a reliable object of worship according to this psalm? Find all that you can.

DAY 5

Helping the Next Generation

Elementary school, as challenging as it can be for girls' relationships, can seem like a sparkling blue swimming pool with a friendly lifeguard compared to the crocodile-infested swamp of middle school. Now one must navigate through a maze of classrooms, teachers, and students. The aggression of adolescent girls tends to be hidden, unlike the open physical aggression of boys. A girl knows that paddling her raft through the dark swamp of middle school can be treacherous.

Not only must we coach our daughters and young friends to deal with depravity in others, we must help them deal with it in themselves. Mothers attending an in-depth Bible conference in Tennessee were awakened to the depravity in their daughters when *Mean Girls* author Haley DiMarco came back to the arena to address them after leading a workshop for their fourteen- to seventeen-year-old daughters. When DiMarco asked these girls how many had had a mean girl in their lives, most of their hands went up. When she asked them how many had been a mean girl, not only did most of the hands go up, but a cheer went out. Shocked, she spoke sternly to the girls and then went to their mothers, pleading for their help. At that particular retreat, there was repentance on the part of the girls, and truly, a beautiful outcome.

I was impressed at how my friend Connie trained her daughter Andrea in a difficult friendship situation. Andrea's best friend had gotten the lead in a school play and seemed to have little time for Andrea. She had new friends, a new schedule, and Andrea felt left in the dust. Instead of telling Andrea exactly what to do, Connie told her daughter to ask God for wisdom and then to do what He told her to do.

"How will He tell me?" Andrea asked.

"I don't know." Connie said. "He often speaks through the Bible—so it might be when you are reading your Bible, or He might bring a verse to mind—or He might speak to you through a person. I don't know. But He promises that He will give wisdom if we ask. So ask—wait—be alert."

For three days, Andrea asked God. She kept telling Connie: "He's not showing me." Connie said, confidently, "He will. I don't know when and I don't know how. But He will."

One day Andrea came down to breakfast and said, "He spoke to me."

"How?"

"This morning, I was reading Proverbs 17:17. It says, "A friend loves at all times." That's a verse I memorized in Awana—and it was like it was highlighted, underlined, and in bold when I read it this morning."

Connie not only taught Andrea how to respond to her friend, but also she taught her how to seek God.

20. What are some ways that a mother (or a mentor) might guide her daughter to take wise paths in friendship?

21. If you read chapter 3 in *The Friendships of Women,* what stood out to you?

The most significant way to overcome clinging too tightly to anyone or anything under the sun is to become a true worshiper of God. Often this is passed on, not by telling, but by showing.

22. As you reflect on your life, do you see any of these qualities growing in you as a worshiper?

   A. Your heart pants for the living God.

   B. In the morning you make your requests and wait upon Him.

   C. You run in the path of His commands, and He has set your heart free.

   D. You are not anxious in the time of drought.

E. You hold people and things under the sun loosely, for God is meeting your deepest needs.

23. Has this week's study impressed anything particular on you that could lead to a personal prayer request? Write down a sentence concerning that, or concerning another personal need, that you would be willing to lift up in prayer.

PRAYER TIME

Cluster in groups of three or four. Have each woman lift up her answer to question 21 in prayer, and then allow the others to support her. When there is a pause, another woman should lift up her need.

Four

Relational Idolatry

Sometimes friends are a surprise gift from God. Rachel, an energetic and witty young woman, has been that for me. I was drawn to her initially because of her lifestyle of radical obedience. She and her husband, though newlyweds, were regularly practicing biblical hospitality. They had befriended their neighbors and now had a neighborhood beginner's Bible study. They had a mentally retarded foster child. And they were always the ones who would invite newcomers home with them for Sunday dinner. I was curious as to how a twenty-five-year-old who did not grow up in a Christian home became so mature, so I invited Rachel out for lunch. As often happens with the Lord, when you put your hand in His and let Him lead you in friendship, He has more for you than you ever could have imagined. Such was the case with Rachel. I had no idea that she had been set free of the practice of homosexuality and that she would make such a vital contribution to my writing of *The Friendships of Women*. Rachel's story opened my eyes. Not only did she help me understand how someone could be tempted by homosexuality, but she also helped me recognize the astonishing truth that the root problem of lesbians is similar to a problem most women struggle with: relational idolatry.

DAY I

Growing in Compassion

Prepare your heart by praying verbatim with your whole heart through this passage:

Teach me, O LORD, to follow your decrees;
then I will keep them to the end.

Give me understanding, and I will keep your law
and obey it with all my heart.

Direct me in the path of your commands,
   for there I find delight.

Turn my heart toward your statutes
   and not toward selfish gain.

Psalm 119:33-36

As we headed toward my favorite restaurant, a cozy place with booths, candles, and the smell of homemade soup, Rachel casually asked me what I was presently writing. When I told her it was a book on the friendships of women, she gasped. I looked at her curiously. At first, she dodged. "There's a need for that book, and I would definitely read it." I wasn't satisfied. I knew, intuitively, that there was more behind her startled reaction. Beseechingly, my eyes met hers. After a minute she responded. "Just give me a little time to gather my courage and I'll tell you." She took a deep breath. "I think the Lord must have arranged for us to have this time together, so I'll tell you," she promised. "I will."

Rachel was so nervous—I really couldn't imagine what she was going to tell me. We waited until we'd both ordered, and then Rachel took the plunge: "I was in a lesbian relationship in college."

I could tell Rachel was watching me to see how I'd respond. I knew, from other friends who have been delivered of these chains, that they are very careful who they tell, for the church's record is mighty poor in showing compassion to those who have struggled or are struggling with this sin. I grabbed Rachel's hands and thanked her for trusting me so quickly.

Before we even look at what the Scripture has to say about homosexuality, I want to address the fact that while many in the body of Christ have been compassionate and have served in caring ministries that help those with AIDS or those who have practiced homosexuality, many other Christians have not been compassionate. They have lacked sensitivity through harshness or jesting. Within your small group, there may be tremendous pain because of the chains of homosexuality, and so we must begin by addressing our own compassion.

WARMUP

In there an area in your life where you lacked compassion but, through suffering, have become more compassionate?

1. Read 2 Corinthians 1:4-7.

   A. How is God described in verse 3?

   B. According to verse 4, in which troubles will He comfort us and why?

C. Do you think if our troubles are a result of our own sins that God will still comfort us? (See Luke 15:11-20.)

D. Share a personal example of how God has shown you that a behavior was wrong yet still was merciful and compassionate toward you.

2. Read Galatians 6:1-5.

A. In verse 1, what pain is expressed in the phrase "overtaken in a trespass?" Can you relate? Is there an area where you have ever been or are now "overtaken in a trespass?" If so, describe the pain.

B. According to verse 1, in what kind of spirit are we to attempt restoring our brothers? Imagine that you are in chains of a food, substance, or sexual addiction. What kind of approach do you think would increase your receptivity? What might decrease your receptivity?

C. Why are we to have a spirit of gentleness? (vs. 1-4)

When we compare ourselves to other people, we may feel superior. But verse three reminds us that truly, that superior feeling is deceptive. We must compare ourselves to Christ, be rightly humbled, and then we will have compassion for others, no matter what their struggle may be.

Understanding some of the factors leading to homosexuality can also help us grow in grace. Counselors have identified several situations that seem to make a woman more vulnerable to the temptation of homosexuality. Childhood sexual abuse is a common component in many lesbians. A girl who is abused by a man is understandably going to be repulsed by men sexually. Because of the deterioration of the family and the easy access to child pornography on the internet, sexual abuse is rampant. One study found that one-third of the women who had been abused sexually as children by males were in a homosexual lifestyle as adults. Other common factors are having a mother who is disrespectful of her husband (influencing the daughters to disrespect men) and/or having a cold, indifferent mother (influencing daughters to yearn for motherly affection). Rachel's history revealed two of these components. Speaking slowly and hesitatingly, she said:

I don't know how it happened. I know my vulnerability was increased by sexual abuse from an uncle. He made me do things I wouldn't consider doing in my marriage. I also know I had a deep need for affirmation from a woman. And homosexual relationships between women are different in character from homosexual relationships between men. In my opinion, men have such strong physical urges that the priority is often sexual. But with women, there is a nurturing tenderness which can seem deceptively beautiful.

But I don't want to give the idea that you have to be either a victim of abuse or of a cold mother to be tempted by homosexuality. I truly think it could happen to anyone who doesn't have God as first place in her life.

Scripture confirms Rachel's words. The root sin, according to the passage we will look at in Romans, is worshiping a person instead of God. Scripture clearly says practicing homosexuality is sin and also gives hope that the truth can set anyone in bondage free.

I have had women come up to me after I have spoken on the friendships of women at retreats and tell me that they do not see a conflict between their practice of lesbianism and Christianity. There are churches who twist the Scriptures, polluting God's clear warning. They also will say that it is unloving to stand against the practice of homosexuality because it could be that some are born with a genetic tendency toward homosexuality. The jury is still out on that point, but it could be that just as some have a genetic tendency toward alcoholism or violence, some have a genetic tendency toward homosexuality. We are also discovering the power of generational sin, and what it really means for the sins of the fathers to be passed on to the next generation. That does not mean, however, that even if we were born with tendencies, that they cannot be overcome, for God doesn't give us commands that are impossible to obey. It is more difficult, for example, for a person with a predisposition toward alcoholism not to fall into that bondage, but neither does he or she have to be an alcoholic. We would direct such a person to a twelve-step program and know that he or she could be set free.

As a matter of fact, our predisposition toward sin is embedded deep within all of us. I was born with a propensity to greed, to lying, to selfishness, and to all kinds of sin. I lied before I could walk, I stole nickels from my mother's purse when I was a first-grader, and my favorite topic of conversation was (and often still is) myself. I can't imagine anyone accepting this statement from me: "This is the way I was born. I must be true to who I really am. Don't ask me to deny my nature. I am a liar, a thief, and I must be focused continually on myself. Accept me as I am!" Instead, I know that denying myself is my only hope. I die daily so that the Holy Spirit can flourish in me. I don't have to be in bondage to sin. Writer for *World,* Andrew Seu, writes that "sin runs deeper than we thought. Like the mildewed cloth that the Mosaic law threw on the pyre, 'What a wretched man I am!' Paul exclaims upon discovering this (Rom. 7:24–25). 'Who will deliver me from this body of death? Thanks be to God through Jesus Christ our Lord.'" God abundantly supplies the resources we need to abstain from sin, even sin that is embedded in us from the womb.

Satan is a master deceiver. The three lies he tells most frequently to those caught in this lifestyle are: "You are not really sinning"; "You can never change"; and "You will not be happy if you leave this lifestyle." God's Word is clear. The practice of homosexuality is sin, and you can be free. I know women who were in deep bondage to this practice who have not only been set free but are also filled with His great joy and peace.

3. What sin or sins, embedded in you from the womb, do you have hope of being free from because of the power of Jesus Christ?

4. If you can identify with bondage, whether it is sexual immorality, gluttony, a bad temper, or something else, what approaches might be helpful from your sisters in helping you get free? What approach might not?

DAY 2
. . . .

The Root Sin

Reflectively, Rachel said:

> *I had a void in my life. I didn't understand that that void was created in me to be filled with God, so I turned to Laura. We began to spend too much time together—taking walks, drinking and partying together, talking into the wee hours of the morning. We began to rely on each other for everything. I see now that's when Satan got a foothold. Everything became a blur as we focused completely on each other: college, our studies, our goals for graduation, fellow students—none of that was important. All that mattered was each other.... My love for Laura kept growing. I was shocked to find myself longing to hold her. Just put my arms around her.*

> *I'll never forget the night. We'd been drinking, playing cards, feeling loose. At one point I looked up at Laura and we exchanged a penetrating look that ripped my heart. I felt the beauty of love and the pain of passion. I knew what was going to happen.*

> *After the first night, I felt so ashamed. It was hard to face Laura the next day when we were both sober. We both apologized to the other and attributed it to being drunk out of our gourds. I wanted to believe it would never happen again, but on the other hand, I wanted it to.*

> *There was a soul-wrenching misery I could not deny.*

> *We'd been drinking heavily one night, when suddenly Laura broke down, sobbing uncontrollably. She completely floored me by telling me that our relationship was going to result in eternal suffering in hell. I didn't know what to say. I was stunned. When Laura had been a junior-high student, at a youth retreat, she had committed her life to Christ. I had seen Laura with her Bible, and I thought it was kind of neat. But she hadn't talked to me about spiritual truths—until that night. Then she poured out her testimony and showed me the Scriptures.*

A kaleidoscope of emotions poured through me—the intense fear of losing Laura, the shame of sin, and the hope of deliverance. I knew she was serious about changing when she told me she had booked a flight to Sarasota over Spring Break. A strong Christian couple down there had offered to help her. She hoped, she told me weeping, "they will help me straighten out my life, because I can't do it myself."

In God's uncanny timing, I had planned to spend my Spring Break at a journalism seminar in nearby Tampa. When Laura's Christian friends realized Rachel was so close, they invited me down for counsel as well. During that time, both of us surrendered our lives fully to Christ: me for the first time, and Laura in recommitment. The day that I dropped to my knees, I promised Jesus that if He would deliver me from the mess I was in, I would turn around and glorify Him. Someday, I vowed, I would help others who were in the same bondage.

The road to healing was not without pain. We were not instantly delivered from our desire for each other. We stumbled and fell a few times, but there was no joy in the sin anymore. Counselors advised a time of separation, and we obeyed. Laura moved to another part of the country. Despite the initial pain of obedience, we both longed for full deliverance. We longed for normal lives with husbands and children. During that time we kept in touch by letter and phone.

There were times when I didn't think I'd get over Laura. There were times I thought I might fall into it with someone else. But, slowly, as I chose to obey, I knew God was doing a work in my heart. In time, the overwhelming feelings I had for Laura, I learned to have in an uplifting way for Christ.

Today we are each happily married to wonderful men, serving the Lord, and good friends. I am keeping my promise and working with other women who are in the bondage of lesbianism. If they've lived in this lifestyle a long time, their chains are tight. They also have to deal with tremendous pressure from their partner and from the gay community not to change. That's why a move can be so helpful. I want to give these women hope. Christ can break chains if you are determined to obey. I now know that our friendship became unbalanced when we began to look to each other for the fulfillment of our lives. Every day, I need to choose to keep Christ as the first and foremost focus of my life.

5. What stood out to you from Rachel and Laura's story? What principles for overcoming bondage did you see?

Read Romans 1:18-23 in the *Amplified Bible*:

[18]*For God's [holy] wrath and indignation are revealed from heaven against all ungodliness and unrighteousness of men, who in their wickedness repress and hinder the truth and make it inoperative.*

¹⁹For that which is known about God is evident to them and made plain in their inner consciousness, because God [Himself] has shown it to them.

²⁰For ever since the creation of the world His invisible nature and attributes, that is, His eternal power and divinity, have been made intelligible and clearly discernible in and through the things that have been made (His handiworks). So [men] are without excuse [altogether without any defense or justification],

²¹Because when they knew and recognized Him as God, they did not honor and glorify Him as God or give Him thanks. But instead they became futile and godless in their thinking [with vain imaginings, foolish reasoning, and stupid speculations] and their senseless minds were darkened.

²²Claiming to be wise, they became fools [professing to be smart, they made simpletons of themselves].

²³And by them the glory and majesty and excellence of the immortal God were exchanged for and represented by images, resembling mortal man and birds and beasts and reptiles.

6. According to Romans 1:18, what truth have people repressed and hindered?

7. Why, according to verses 19 and 20, are people without excuse? See also Psalm 19:1-4.

8. What, according to verse 21, did people fail to do? What was the result?

9. What did they then do, according to verses 22-23?

In closing today, pray through Psalm 119:37-40, praying for revival in the church and in your own heart.

Turn my eyes away from worthless things;
preserve my life according to your word.

Fulfill your promise to your servant,
so that you may be feared.

Take away the disgrace I dread,
for your laws are good.

> *How I long for your precepts!*
> *Preserve my life in your righteousness.*

DAY 3
. . . .

The Downward Spiral

It is frightening to see the repeated phrase in the passage we will continue in today: "God gave them over..." The root sin, if not repented of, gives Satan a foothold. Then there is a downward spiral in which Satan's grasp becomes stronger and stronger. Soon we are not only deeply entrenched in the sin personally, but we encourage others in it too. This can be seen with many sins, and in homosexuality, there is definitely a "gay agenda" that affects our children through media and public schools. Young people are encouraged to experiment sexually with the same sex to see if they might be gay. Counselor John White writes, "Once I experience physical pleasure with a member of my own sex, I am more likely to want to experience it again. The more frequently I experience it, the more fixed the pattern will become."

Read Romans 1:24-35.

10. Find the first judgment of God in verse 24.

11. Find the root sin repeated in verse 25.

12. Find the second "God gave them over" in verse 26.

13. What the result, according to verse 27?

14. Find the third "God gave them over" in verse 28.

15. What final downward step is described in verse 32?

16. If you have a son or a daughter approaching adolescence, you would be wise to discuss some of the myths about homosexuality. The following are some examples you may want to discuss. Consider roleplaying with your daughter, helping her to articulate the truth back in defense.

    A. You may be gay and you don't know it. Experimenting with the same sex will help you to know.

B. If you have a predisposition toward homosexuality this is the way you must always be.

C. It is not loving to tell someone that the practice of homosexuality is wrong. The Bible tells us not to judge.

D. David and Jonathan were homosexuals, and God was pleased with them.

For more information, I recommend: *The Truth about Same-Sex Marriage* by Erwin Lutzer. Also see Leader's Helps, p. 168.

Pray through this entire octrain for yourself, and for a young person in your life from Psalm 119.

May your unfailing love come to me, O LORD,
your salvation according to your promise;

then I will answer the one who taunts me,
for I trust in your word.

Do not snatch the word of truth from my mouth,
for I have put my hope in your laws.

I will always obey your law,
for ever and ever.

I will walk about in freedom,
for I have sought out your precepts.

I will speak of your statutes before kings
and will not be put to shame,

for I delight in your commands
because I love them.

I lift up my hands to your commands, which I love,
and I meditate on your decrees.

Psalm 119:41-48

DAY 4

Relational Idolatry Doesn't Have to Be Sexual

You don't have to be in a homosexual lifestyle to be caught in the bondage of relational idolatry. It can happen between a boyfriend and girlfriend, husband and wife, or simply two close friends of the same sex.

Christy is a very capable professional woman who has had a personal relationship with the Lord from a young age. Yet her friendships were not healthy. Christy told me:

> *It was a cyclical pattern for me to cling too tightly to my girlfriends. For example, the friendship I was in when I finally began to realize my problem was with Brooke. We communicated a lot through e-mail, and she would e-mail me during her breaks at work. I knew her schedule well, so if I didn't hear my computer say, "YOU'VE GOT MAIL," I'd become anxious. I'd wonder, "Have I done something wrong?" I'd e-mail her—and I wouldn't quit until I received a response. My anxiety would heighten when a third party, like a boyfriend, would come into the picture. I felt like our relationship was threatened, and it would affect me physically. I actually felt like I had the flu—my stomach was so frequently upset.*

Because Christy was involved in the body of Christ, she had healthy friends who were concerned about her and began to talk to her. "My friends said to me, 'This is a pattern in you. Your response isn't healthy. You need to get help.' One friend even called me with the phone number of a good counselor and told me to make an appointment because she'd be calling me back to see if I had. So, I did."

> *It was through my counselor that I first became aware of the term "relational idolatry." As soon as she said the phrase, I knew it was a correct diagnosis, suddenly helping me understand that I was sinning against God. I was worshiping a person. I was doing a Beth Moore study—Breaking Free—and studying about the kings that wouldn't take down the high places. They worshiped idols. I thought, That's me! I wrote Brooke and told her, "I can't explain it now, but I am realizing I need help. I can't e-mail or talk to you while I am getting counseling." She tried to understand, but it was difficult for her. Eventually I was able to explain and she not only understood, but also was thankful. Today our friendship is healthy and restored. I just helped Brooke put together a slide show for her wedding reception. We had a great time talking about her upcoming marriage and plans for me to visit them. After I was in counseling for six months, I spent another eighteen months doing a lot of reading and Bible study on the subject of codependency. I truly am free. My friendships are healthy and restored. I have a joy, peace, and a much deeper relationship with the Lord. He came and filled the void that I had been trying, unsuccessfully, to fill with friends.*

17. What stood out to you from Christy's story?

18. What principles for overcoming bondage do you see in Christy's story?

Any relationship, even a relationship between a boyfriend and girlfriend or husband and wife can involve relational idolatry. Any time you are looking to a person for what only God can be, you are in a danger zone. In *Emotional Dependency: A Threat to Close Friendships*, Lori Thorkelson Rentzel writes: "Whether or not physical involvement exists, sin enters the picture when a friendship becomes a dependent relationship." In a healthy friendship, we desire to see our friend reach her potential—it is a giving friend-ship in which we build her up, encourage her to reach out to others, and find ways to serve God. Though most of us may not feel tempted by homosexuality, I believe the evi-dence is strong that we are tempted by dependency. An emotionally dependent relation-ship produces bondage.

19. Consider the following warning signs Rentzel lists as signs of an emotionally dependent relationship. Are any of them true of you concerning another person?

   - experiences frequent jealousy, possessiveness, and a desire for exclusivism, viewing other people as a threat to the relationship

   - prefers to spend time alone with this friend and becomes frustrated when this does not happen

   - becomes irrationally angry or depressed when this friend withdraws slightly

20. If you see that relational idolatry is a problem in your life, what principles of over-coming bondage could you apply?

DAY 5

Helping One Another Find Strength in God

We are all weak. We are all prone to relational idolatry and its corollary sins: jealousy, possessiveness, and gossip—for gossip too springs from idolatry, for it is a way of say-ing, "You and I are on the inside, but she is on the outside." Solomon tells us that gossip is like "tasty morsels," for when we gossip, there is often laughter, the thrill of connec-tion, and the fleeting feeling of superiority. But then those "tasty morsels" turn to gravel in our mouths for we know, from His Spirit, that we have wounded another and disap-pointed God.

How wonderful if, instead of seeking that fleeting and often fickle delight from a person, we can be steadfast in longing for a lasting treasure—the delight of God. When we put a seal over our lips, refuse to participate in gossip, and instead, help each other find strength in God, the Lord is so pleased.

21. Read Ephesians 5.

   A. What command is given in verse 2? What would this look like as you plan your day?

   B. What should there not be even a hint of and why according to verse 3?

C. What should replace foolish talk according to verse 4? What would this look like in your conversations today?

D. What is the root sin in immorality and greed according to verse 5? What stern warning comes with this? Why, do you think so?

E. How are we to live, according to verse 8, and how is this described according to verses 9–11?

F. A principle of God's is that, as we choose the light, the light grows stronger in us. How can you see this in the quotation from verse 14?

G. What is the secret, according to verse 18, in helping one another find strength in God? How can one be "filled with the Spirit"?

H. Describe some of the ways to help each other find strength in God according to verse 19. Have you experienced this with other believers?

I. What instruction is repeated in verse 20?

22. If you read chapter 4 in *The Friendships of Women*, what stood out to you?

23. Has this week's study impressed anything particular on you that could lead to a personal prayer request? Write down a sentence concerning that request or another personal need that you would be willing to lift up in prayer.

PRAYER TIME

Cluster in groups of three or four. Have each woman lift up her answer to question 23 in prayer, and then allow the others to support her. When there is a pause, another woman should lift up her need.

Five

Naomi: A Female Job

Though there is so much in life that it is wonderful, there is also enormous pain and sorrow. If you haven't experienced great sorrow, you will—for no one escapes. Not only do we need to be prepared for pain ourselves, if we are truly going to be the kind of friend who loves at all times, we must know how to help our sisters in pain. This is an enormous part of our calling in Christ Jesus.

For some, the journey of life is incredibly hard. Naomi has sometimes been called a female Job, for within the first five verses, she experiences more loss than most women will ever know.

When I wrote *The Friendships of Women* originally, I had experienced sorrow, but nothing compared to the earthquakes that lay ahead. I am so much more empathetic with Naomi today. Having lost my own dear life's companion, I understand something of what Simeon meant when he told Mary, "A sword will pierce your soul." Though life goes on, and though there is purpose, hope, and so much to be thankful for, I sometimes think when I am with others, *Can't you see the knife sticking out of my heart?* I've lost the one who loved me more than anyone on earth: my confidante, my protector, and my provider. It has made me appreciate, more than I ever did, the great gift of a good marriage—of being one with another in body and soul.

And yet losing Steve has caused me to turn, with a desperation, to my heavenly Bridegroom, and to trust Him to be my Confidante, my Protector, and my Provider. Single women often can understand this in a way married women can only imagine.

There comes a time when Naomi, like Job, despairs, not of God, but of life on this earth. She cries, "Don't call me Naomi [sweet or pleasant]...call me Mara [bitter]." But as the story continues, I see the warmth of Ruth's love thawing Naomi's frozen heart. I see Ruth's faith in God begin to restore Naomi's faith and help her to see what was always there: His unfailing love.

That's what sisters in Christ who are true worshipers of God can do for their sisters in pain. As a woman worships God, His strength and His Spirit pours into her. Then she can be His arms, His heart, and His love to her sister who is overburdened.

DAY I

A Female Job

WARMUP

Share a time when you were genuinely hurting and a friend helped you. What did she do?

Consider why Naomi has sometimes been called a female Job.

1. The opening verse is packed with the premonition of sorrow. Read each phrase, and then read the passage in parenthesis. What light does the history, in each case, lend?

   A. "In those days Israel had no king" (Judg. 21:25).

   B. "There was a famine in the land" (Deut. 11:13-18).

   C. "And a man from Bethlehem in Judah, together with his wife and two sons, went to live for a while in the country of Moab."

   1) How did the nation of Moab begin? (Gen. 13:30-37)

   2) The famine of Ruth took place in the days of Judges. Read Judges 3:12-30 and see what clues you can find for wealth in Moab.

   3) While they lived in Moab, Naomi's sons married Moabite women, and this surely must have caused her concern, for they would have worshiped other gods. This pattern of marrying Moabite women was passed on through the generations, for Naomi's great-great-grandson, Solomon, also married Moabite women (among other foreign women)! What happened to him according to 1 Kings 3:1-4? What else did Solomon do according to 1 Kings 3:11?

   The gods of Moab were Chemosh and Molech, who demanded sexual immorality in the temple and the sacrifice of babies on the altar.

   4) What was the reputation of Moab, according to Isaiah 16:6?

5) As you learn about Moab, what do you think about Elimelech's decision to move his family there?

6) What choices have you made that look good short-term but have long-term negative consequences?

2. Look carefully in Ruth 1 and pull out any phrases of sorrow. Look for phrases such as "was left with," "barren," "empty," "bitter," etc.

3. Why do you think Naomi is sometimes called a female Job?

Both Job and Naomi suffered far more than most individuals, losing all of their family, all of their wealth. Satan was the instigator of Job's suffering, though God allowed it. Satan's taunt to God was that Job trusted God only because of what God gave him. One of the primary lessons in the book of Job is "Will you trust the Lord even if He doesn't bless you? Will you love Him because of who He is and not because of what He gives?" Job certainly passed the test with memorable statements of faith:

Naked came I out of my mother's womb, and naked shall I return thither: the LORD gave, and the LORD hath taken away; blessed be the name of the LORD.

Job 1:21 (KJV)

Though he slay me, yet will I trust in him…

Job 13:15 (KJV)

Both Job and Naomi trusted God, yet were worn down as the suffering continued. Naomi was able to be loving and filled with grace toward her Moabite daughters-in-law, even after losing her husband, her home, and her hope of having daughters-in-law who shared her faith. But when she loses her sons, she begins to despair of life. She doesn't turn her back on God, but she bewails the bitterness of her life.

4. Find phrases that show the despair of each of their hearts in the following passages:

Job 23   Ruth 1:11-21

61

> *For the view of the Bible is that it is far better to be sincerely discouraged and world-weary than to pretend enthusiasm, better to be authentically sad than artificially happy, better to have honest doubt than phony faith.*
>
> Mike Mason, *The Gospel According to Job*

5. Can you also find, in the above passages or elsewhere in their stories, any evidence that Job and Naomi still reverenced God?

6. Despite her pain and despite the fact that she is sending her daughters-in-law back to Moab, tenderness can still be seen in her words in Ruth 1:8-9. How does she affirm them? How does she pray for them?

7. Remembering the theme of the land in the book of Ruth and its parallel to the hearts of God's people, what hope do you see in the last verse of Ruth 1?

DAY 2

Hope in the Midst of Despair

Though we do not meet Naomi until the bottom drops out of her life, and though she is not particularly pleasant at that point, we can glean much about her character from the way her daughters-in-law responded to her. There must have been something very pleasant about Naomi for these girls to be willing to give up their homes, people, and families in order to move to Bethlehem with Naomi. Though it would be reasonable to suspect that they were not, as Moabites, her dream daughters-in-law, she must have still loved them well. Perhaps she tried to dissuade her sons from marrying Moabites, but once they did, she chose to love her Moabite daughters-in-law. Ruth was drawn, not only to Naomi but, eventually, to Naomi's God.

After losing her sons, Naomi goes through a period of bitterness. But before that, she still has hope in the midst of despair. She must have still been breathing truth into her soul as we see Job do.

How do we have hope in the midst of despair? We remind ourselves of God's unchanging promises despite the difficulty of our present circumstances. Today's octrain from Psalm 119 will show you how to do this. When I was writing my study guide on the Psalms (now titled *A Woman of Worship*) I worked with Integrity Music, for there is a musical CD in this guide with the psalms studied set to music. Integrity sent me dozens of "Psalm Songs," but the one that came to mean the most to me and my husband was one based on the opening two verses of this octrain. Meditate on them in the following two versions:

> *Remember the word to Your servant,*
> *Upon which You have caused me to hope.*
> *This is my comfort in my affliction,*
> *For Your word has given me life.*
>
> **Psalm 119:49-50 (NKJV)**
>
> *Remember what you said to me, your servant—*
> *I hang on to these words for dear life!*
>
> *These words hold me up in bad times;*
> *yes, your promises rejuvenate me.*
> **Psalm 119:49-50 (MSG)**

8. How, according to the above passage, does the psalmist find hope in the midst of despair?

Job clung to this: *For I know that my redeemer liveth, and that he shall stand at the latter day upon the earth* (Job 19:25 KJV). How amazing to see that the Spirit of the living God helped Job, one of the earliest men who ever lived, to know about Jesus—and that Job himself would one day see him standing on the earth!

I cling to this promise as well, and to the promise that my husband will have (or has now) a resurrection body, and that one day there will be no more pain, no more tears, and no more death. I also cling to and remind God of His promises to be a husband to the widow, a Father to the fatherless, and a Comforter who will never leave me or forsake me.

9. What pain are you facing now? What two specific promises could you breathe into your soul from God's Word that would give you hope in the midst of despair?

10. Now, consider some of your dearest friends who may be facing sorrow or pain right now. What hope could you give them through the promises of God?

11. Pray responsively through the entire octrain:

Remember your word to your servant,
for you have given me hope.

My comfort in my suffering is this:
Your promise preserves my life.

The arrogant mock me without restraint,
but I do not turn from your law.

*I remember your ancient laws, O L*ORD*,*
> *and I find comfort in them.*

Indignation grips me because of the wicked,
> *who have forsaken your law.*

Your decrees are the theme of my song
> *wherever I lodge.*

*In the night I remember your name, O L*ORD*,*
> *and I will keep your law.*

This has been my practice:
> *I obey your precepts.*

Psalm 119:50-56

DAY 3

A Woman's Tendency toward Dependency

It's easier to see that Rachel was wrong in making another woman her source of joy and security than to look at Naomi and say she was foolish to do the same thing with her husband. For those of us raised on Cinderella, not trusting in your husband, especially if he is a good man, may be a new thought.

I look back now to a conversation I had nearly twenty years ago with our then ten-year-old daughter, Sally and her friend, Tricia. When I read this conversation now, as a new widow, I realize God was preparing me to depend on Him instead of my husband.

Sally and Tricia were practically joined at the hip. They zipped their sleeping bags together, shared their popsicles, and even, when pressed, borrowed each other's underwear and toothbrushes. When they were separated, I sensed Sally's anxiety. They told me they would absolutely die if they didn't get in the same fifth grade. Pondering their friendship, I asked, "Do you think you are dependent on each other?"

"What does dependent mean?" Tricia asked.

Searching quickly for a simple synonym, I said, "Do you think you need each other?"

In unison they chimed, "YES!"

Seeing my perturbed pause, Sally questioned, "Is that bad?"

"Well," I responded, "we should be dependent on Jesus."

"Can't I be dependent on Jesus and Tricia?" my daughter asked.

I considered this. (I, who had recently told my extremely capable tax-form-filler-outer, smoke-alarm-putter-upper, sliver-remover husband that if anything happened to him, I hoped a total-care nursing home would accept a forty-two-year-old woman with her three children, contemplated this.) Finally I told Sally, who was waiting expectantly: "I think we both have some growing up to do. It's important to love our friends, to cherish them, and to be committed to them. Girls and women are good at that, and it's a beautiful side to our friendships. But we need to learn to be dependent, leaning on God, because He's the only one who will never betray us, die, or move away."

Sally looked at me quizzically. She could not imagine any of these things destroying her friendship with Tricia. I, too, never dreamed Steve would die in his fifties and that I would have to live without him. When I hear LeAnn Rimes sing "How can I live without you, how can I breathe without you ..." I so understand. And yet I know that those kinds of thoughts are only rightly directed to Jesus.

God saw my future and knew I would have to live without Steve. So He began to speak the truth gently to me. *Depend on Me, Dee—I am the only One who is the Solid Rock.*

I so understand Naomi's devastation. I even understand her misguided attempt to get her daughters-in-law married off to unbelieving Moabite men. As women, sometimes our god is marriage, and we will do whatever to get it for ourselves or others! How we need to be women who cherish people: friends, husbands, and children—but who depend only on God.

12. Consider again the "parting scene" between Naomi and her daughters-in-law, for there is more to see.

    A. Count how many times Naomi sends her daughters-in-law back to Moab in Ruth 1:8-18.

    B. What reasons does she give for sending them back? Why, from an eternal perspective, might it have been better not to let them come to Bethlehem? What fears, do you think, might have clouded her thinking?

    C. Where do you think Naomi's security was at this point, and why?

    In Naomi's day, women were truly destitute without a man. They could not own property but were dependent on their fathers, husbands, or sons to care for them. Yet even then, God longed for women to put their trust in Him. Ruth did, as we will see, and God met her.

13. Do you think your security is in the Lord or somewhere else? Ask God to search your heart, and be honest with yourself.

Pray responsively through the next octrain in Psalm 119:

You are my portion, O LORD;
  I have promised to obey your words.

I have sought your face with all my heart;
  be gracious to me according to your promise.

I have considered my ways
  and have turned my steps to your statutes.

I will hasten and not delay
  to obey your commands.

Though the wicked bind me with ropes,
  I will not forget your law.

At midnight I rise to give you thanks
  for your righteous laws.

I am a friend to all who fear you,
  to all who follow your precepts.

The earth is filled with your love, O LORD;
  teach me your decrees.

Psalm 119:57-64

DAY 4

Don't Push Your Friends Away

Luci Shaw, my friend and favorite poet, was widowed in midlife. She described being widowed as "radical surgery—like being cut in half." When Luci lost her husband, she lived in a wooded suburb of Chicago. One day we walked together in her front yard and looked at the place where a large oak tree had stood. A week or so after her husband had died, the tree, ridden with disease, had to be toppled. In her freshly widowed pain, Luci had seen parallels between the screaming power saws and her husband's cancer and the white-hot fire that burned the debris and stump for two days after his death. Finally, she herself identified with the black-rimmed ashen hole that was left like a wound in the frozen sod. As we stood there silently, I recalled words she'd written in an article:

  I was the frozen sod with the deep wound, and Harold was my tree who was simply ...
  gone. Vanished. How unreal it seemed that his roots, that had for over thirty years pene-
  trated deep into my life, that had anchored us, joined us so solidly and securely, were

being eroded by the fire of decay. The space above ground that for so long had been filled with his vertical strength and solidity and shape was empty; air had rushed in where, before, the towering trunk had outbranched to leaves. Now I lie in wait for spring, for the tissue of earth and the skin of sod—the beauty of green instead of the grey ashes of a spent fire—to fill in and heal over the naked scar. And it will. It will. But the oak tree stands strong and thriving and leafy in my memory, and no one can cut it down.

When Naomi was widowed, she tried to send her daughters-in-law away. Luci understood that even though there is a temptation to pull the blanket over your head in grief and to send everyone away, that she needed her friends desperately. In support of this conviction, Luci showed me her calendar, dotted with time for friends. "It doesn't take much time to go out for breakfast," she commented. "It doesn't interfere with one's work schedule. I need to make time for that contact. I would feel much more bereft without my friends."

In times of grief, we are apt to hear dark voices—voices that tell us we are no longer people of value, beloved by God. If we withdraw from friends, a common response to depression, then those voices have no competition. We need to be with compassionate women who come alongside and show us that we are lovable, precious in God's sight and in their sight. If our friends don't come to be with us, we must ask for their company. Luci does this. She and author Karen Mains are good friends. Luci said: I'll call Karen, and say, "Do you feel like going to a matinee?" and she'll say, "Oh, I've been writing all weekend! Let's go!"

That does wonders for me. It takes my mind off myself, and in the company of a friend we can see a meaningful movie. Research by Daniel Levinson of Yale indicates that difficult times in life, such as midlife or the loss of a mate, are more successfully negotiated by those who have strong same-sex friendships. That is why women seem to cope better than men with the loss of a spouse. Dr. Beth Hess says, "There is a strong hypothesis that friends help women survive. Part of women's ability to sustain themselves in older years depends on their capacity for constructing a network of friends."

14. What stood out to you from Luci Shaw's testimony?

15. Luci talks about hearing dark voices in grief, voices that say we are not loved by God, not valuable. What dark voices did Naomi seem to be hearing? (Ruth 1:11-13)

16. When you have experienced grief or depression, have you been tempted to hole up, to push your friends away, as Naomi did? What do you remember?

17. Read Ruth's famous promise in Ruth 1:16-17. How did her words compete with Naomi's dark voices?

18. Luci made breakfast dates or went to a matinee with a friend. What are some simple ways that you can reach out to friends?

19. Read Ecclesiastes 4:9-12. Find everything you can in this passage for the value of a friend.

Naomi seemed to overvalue men and undervalue women. In an article on the book of Ruth, Jane Titterington writes,

> *We need to be reminded that our value as human beings is something bestowed on us by God regardless of our marital status. Placing an inordinate value on the man-woman relationship tends to produce a rather warped view of humanity.... We see men as prey and other women as pawns to be used or rivals to be competed against in this game.*

20. Do you think that you see women as equal in value to men? What do your actions reveal?

DAY 5

Don't Turn Your Back on God

In *Anne of Green Gables,* Anne tells Marilla that she is in "the depths of despair." Then, hoping for empathy, she asks, "Marilla—aren't you ever in the depths of despair?"

Marilla answers firmly, "No. Because to despair is to turn your back on God."

Though Marilla is a bit stern here, still, there is truth in her words. God welcomes us to pour out our hearts to Him, but we are to be slow to anger with the Almighty, for He is holy and good. Often, when the mountains cave in, we display our anger by turning our back on Him, thinking, *He didn't do what I so longed for Him to do, so I'm going to turn away. I'm not going to read His Word, be with His people, or seek Him anymore. I will find another means of comfort.*

When we turn our back on God, we are cutting off our lifeline. How much better to wait on Him, to seek His face, and to trust Him. Though life is painful, God is good, God is in control, and He will do all things well in His time. I love this line, though I do not know who first said it:

It will be okay in the end, and if it isn't okay, it isn't the end.

True worshipers of God hold on to God, even in their deepest grief, trusting His heart. They are honest with Him, telling Him of their grief. Of course we shouldn't pretend, for The Almighty can read our thoughts. True worshipers are honest and persistent in pleading for His help. All of the friends we are studying suffered and pled with God to answer. God always does, but for some, it isn't until heaven. The author of Hebrews writes about those who did not receive their reward on earth, but promises "something better" in the life to come. Naomi and Job suffered long, and much of their pain could not be wiped out on earth. But God did reward each of them and bless them. And we have no idea of their blessing in heaven.

It is interesting to see how God communicates with these saints. They were honest with God, crying out to Him, pleading with Him to show up. God always did, in His time, but He didn't always respond the way the individuals hoped. Habakkuk, for example, cried out about the suffering of Israel. God responded by telling him to expect much more suffering before God turned on Israel's invaders. Like a true worshiper, Habakkuk bowed before God, saying:

I heard and my heart pounded,

my lips quivered at the sound;

Yet I will wait patiently for the day of calamity

to come on the nation invading us.

Though the fig tree does not bud

and there are no grapes on the vines,

though the olive crop fails

and the fields produce no food,

though there are no sheep in the pen

and no cattle in the stalls,

yet I will rejoice in the LORD,

I will be joyful in God my Savior.

   Habakkuk 3:16-18

Likewise, Job said, "Though He slay me, yet will I trust Him." Part of Job's suffering was through the misapplied wisdom of his friends. This is one significant way Naomi's life was different than Job's—Naomi had Ruth, who stood by her side, comforting her, refusing to assume that she knew why Naomi was suffering. Job's friends, in contrast, assumed that Job had sinned. And though the things they said would have been true if Job's suffering were a result of sin, they were off base. Job's suffering was due to Satan, who was seeing if Job truly loved God for Himself and not because God had blessed him. Eventually, God shows up in a dazzling way, silencing not only Job, but also his friends. God also shows up for Naomi, not through a direct encounter like Job, but through people and circumstances.

21. If you read chapter 4 of *The Friendships of Women*, what stood out to you?

22. How do you see Job's honesty with God in the following passages?

    A. Job 29:1-6

    B. Job 30:20-23

    C. Job 31:35

23. When God finally shows up, what are some of the things He says, and how does Job respond?

    A. Job 38:1-7

    B. Job 40:1-5

    C. Job 42:1-6

24. How does God deal with Job's friends? (Job 42:7-9)

When my husband was dying, some came to me in person or through cards with Scripture verses such as Romans 8:28. Though I know Scripture is true, and my friends well-intentioned, hearing sermonettes at that time felt like the knife in my heart was being twisted. What I longed for from my friends was not answers, for I wasn't sure they could know why God was allowing us to suffer so, but for their empathy, prayers, and love. (I wanted a "Ruth," not an "Eliphaz, Bildad, or Zophar.") The cards that ministered most to me were often not store-bought ones but notes that simply told me they were grieving too, that they loved us, and that they would not stop praying for us. Somehow, that cut our pain; whereas, their "scriptural wisdom" often increased our pain.

25. The words that Job's friends spoke were true in general, and we can learn much from them. The problem was that these truths were misapplied to Job. Often suffering is a result of sin, but that wasn't the case for Job. How can we avoid the error of Job's friends?

26. How does God eventually bless Job? (Job 42:10-17)

27. Look at the beginning of Job and find which blessings were doubled and which were not. Do you see any significance in this?

28. How is Naomi honest about her feelings when she is grieving, according to Ruth 1:20-21?

Later, we see hope begin to come to Naomi's heart as God ministers to Ruth through Boaz. When Ruth tells Naomi that she "happened" in the field of Boaz, Naomi says:

"May he be blessed of the LORD who has not withdrawn his kindness to the living and to the dead." Again Naomi said to her, "The man is our relative, he is one of our closest relatives."
                          Ruth 2:20 (NAS)

29. What do you learn about Naomi from the above?

30. Read Ruth 4:9-22 to see how things turned out in the end for Naomi.

    A. Naomi had lost all of her property as a widow. How does that change? (v. 9)

    B. Naomi's late husband's name would have died out since her sons were dead. How does that change? (v. 10)

    C. Describe the prayer of the wedding witnesses. Find three things they ask God for. What do you think each means?

D. Naomi's daughter-in-law Ruth had been barren in Moab. How does this change, and why, as Boaz's wife? (v. 13)

E. What do the women of Bethlehem see happening for Naomi because of the birth of her grandson, Obed? (vs. 14-15)

A kinsman-redeemer is a man related to a woman who will redeem her life by providing for her and protecting her. Obed will grow up to be that for Naomi. Boaz was that for Ruth. (A kinsman-redeemer is a foreshadowing of Christ who is the ultimate Kinsman-Redeemer for His Bride.)

F. How do the women of Bethlehem describe Ruth? (v. 15)

A family of seven sons was considered perfect in Israel.

G. What evidence can you find that Naomi was truly embraced by Ruth and Boaz?

H. How do you see the prayer of verse 12 answered in the genealogy of verses 18-22? In the genealogy of Matthew 1:5-16?

I. From the verses above, what can you learn about the power of godly friends praying for one another?

31. Has this week's study impressed anything particular on you that could lead to a personal prayer request? Write down a sentence concerning that request or another personal need that you would be willing to lift up in prayer.

PRAYER TIME

In groups of three or four, have each woman lift up her answer to question 21 in prayer, and then allow the others to support her. When there is a pause, another woman should lift up her need.

Close with a familiar chorus like "He Is Lord."

Six

Ruth: A Woman Friend

I gladly claim Ruth as a member of my sex. When Naomi was rejecting her, Ruth faced her squarely and said the words that have immortalized her. She makes six promises, and then to convince Naomi she is serious, she calls God's wrath upon her if she doesn't keep them. The loveliness and the gravity of these vows take my breath away. Vows made, not as the composers of wedding music would have us believe, by a bride to her groom, but by one woman to another. What a model of feminine friendship! Ruth shows us the height of which we, as believing women, are capable, for God uses Ruth like a good medicine to restore an ailing Naomi.

DAY I

Six Promises

Naomi keeps urging her daughters-in-law to go back to Moab. She doesn't believe she has anything to offer these women. Her husband is dead, her sons are dead, and her womb "is dead." She tells them, in effect, to "count the cost," for if they come with her, she can't provide husbands for them. She seems convinced that no man from Bethlehem would want a Moabite woman as his wife. Unless they return to Moab, she thinks, they will remain single for the rest of their lives. "Go back," Naomi says, for the third time. At this point, "Orpah kissed her mother-in-law good-bye, but Ruth clung to her" (Ruth 1:14). For a fourth time, Naomi says to Ruth: "Look, your sister-in-law is going back to her people and her gods. Go back with her" (Ruth 1:15). It is then that Ruth makes the speech that has gone down in history—amazing, when you realize she has been told four times to go back. No doubt with tears in her eyes and determination on her whole countenance, Ruth says:

> *Entreat me not to leave thee, or to return from following after thee:*
> *for whither thou goest, I will go; and where thou lodgest,*

74

I will lodge: thy people shall be my people, and thy God my God:

Where thou diest, will I die, and there will I be buried: the LORD do so to me,

and more also, if ought but death part thee and me.

Ruth 1:16-17 (KJV)

WARMUP

Have you ever heard the above passage before? Did you know it was spoken by a daughter-in-law to her mother-in-law? What stands out to you about it and why?

1. Name the six promises that Ruth made to Naomi.

2. Naomi expressed worthlessness, feeling her life was too bitter to share, but Ruth stands against that. What ways do Ruth's actions or words contradict Naomi's clear or probable thoughts, which I have put in bold. (I have my own thoughts in the Leader's Notes, but come up with your own before looking at those!)

   A. Naomi: **Go back to Moab.**

   Ruth?

   B. Naomi: **I do not have value anymore. No man would want me, and even if he did, I can't conceive anymore. I'm empty, worthless, I have nothing to give you...**

   Ruth?

   C. Naomi: **I am not going to be pleasant to be around. Call me Mara.**

   Ruth?

   D. Naomi: **I'm not going to tell you to trust my God. He has dealt severely with me.**

   Ruth?

3. Why do you think Ruth's commitment has become so well known? What about it stands out to you?

4. Why, according to Ruth 1:18, did Naomi stop telling Ruth to go back?

Pray verbatim through Psalm 119:65-68

*Do good to your servant
    according to your word, O LORD.*

*Teach me knowledge and good judgment,
    for I believe in your commands.*

*Before I was afflicted I went astray,
    but now I obey your word.*

*You are good, and what you do is good;
    teach me your decrees.*

DAY 2

Naomi's Response

After I buried my husband in a little church cemetery near our cabin in Wisconsin, I came home to Nebraska. Coming down the driveway, I felt the muscle of my heart grow tight. So often when I'd come home, Steve would be in the garden, and he'd drop everything and come toward the car, smiling. Even after thirty years of marriage, my heart would do a flip when I saw him.

I opened the door to the house. I walked through the rooms, the ache in my heart growing. He wasn't there to greet me, hold me, or ask all the questions that one who truly loves you asks. He'd never lean back on his dining room chair and laugh again, read with me by the fire, or hold me in the night.

He was gone. Yes, I knew, with a greater assurance than Naomi could have known, that one day, because of Jesus and the resurrection, I would see Steve again. I will hold him again, talk to him, and laugh with him. But in this life—never again.

How much better I understand Naomi's pain. As she stood on the hill overlooking Bethlehem, she was hardly aware of Ruth at her side because of the discordant din of pain. Ruth's promises, though they may be the most beautiful words of friendship in all of Scripture, do not evoke a response of appreciation. Not now. Not yet. Naomi is frozen, like the hard ground of winter.

Read Ruth 1:19-22.

5. The "whole town was abuzz." In the Hebrew, there is a feminine plural form for "the whole town," so it was the women "buzzing" with surprise, delight, and concern. Naomi was from a leading family in Bethlehem. She and her three men had been gone ten years. Now she's back with a young woman. Using your imagination, what might have been some of the thoughts and questions from women friends who knew and loved her?

6. How does she respond to, "Can this be Naomi?" Find at least six negative statements.

7. If you had been Ruth, what feelings might you have had at this point? Why?

These are thoughts of one Jewish writer:

> *Her words wound Ruth. Naomi is not alone; Ruth is with her. And how can Naomi's heart be empty when Ruth's own heart brims with love for her? But with the wounding comes the balm of forgiveness. Ruth knows (because Naomi has taught her) that in friendship, one must look away, accept small hurts and probe the source of pain. The source of Naomi's pain is her terrible bereavement, her fear of a solitary and poverty-haunted old age. She has, for the moment, forgotten Ruth, but then she is not infallible. Ruth accepts her as she is, as, indeed, Naomi has always accepted Ruth.*

> Gloria Goldreich, *Reading Ruth*

8. Ruth gives Naomi grace. She doesn't rebuke her or retreat from her, two very natural responses to pain. She silently stands by her side, giving grace. The above author mentions that "Ruth accepts Naomi as she is, as, indeed, Naomi has always accepted Ruth." Do you agree? How has Naomi shown Ruth grace in the past?

9. Often we are better able to give grace and understand someone's hurtful response when we have been in her shoes. Ruth has been widowed as well, so she truly empathizes. Second Corinthians 1:4 says that when we have been comforted by God in an affliction, "we may be able to comfort others." Think of two particular areas where you have suffered or experienced loss. What were your feelings? What helped you? How might you comfort others going through this same valley?

DAY 3

Friends in Grief Need Empathy

When a drunk driver hit her husband's car head-on, Paula's husband and toddler died. In her journal, she wrote:

> *I can't be polite to one more visitor. No one would like me if they knew what I really was thinking when they say how lucky I am that I wasn't badly injured. That I lived. The person I used to be would have understood their intentions.... But today I can't pass off the words. This new person doesn't have energy left to do anything but stay alive and not scream. I don't want to hear anyone else's awkward attempts. They make me angrier than I already am.*

Paula D'Arcy, *Song for Sarah*

I've been that awkward visitor in the hospital room who has wanted so badly to ease my friend's pain that stupid things have tumbled out of my mouth. One of the worst things you can do (and I've done it!) is to point out a silver lining in her storm. She doesn't want to hear how lucky she is!

Sometimes we stay away because of our awkwardness. That is also hurtful. When I was in my twenties, my next-door neighbor, a woman in her forties, died of cancer. At first I visited her regularly; then, because I didn't know what to say, I stopped visiting completely.

Now that I am better acquainted with grief, I know. Go—because all you have to do is stay a few minutes and let them see you hurt for them. Go ahead and cry. Hug them. If you say anything, pray for mercy from God, or tell them you love them and hate what's happening to them. Don't try to fix it. Only God can do that, and if you try, you'll make it worse. When my husband was so sick our friend Lorma would come and put her hand on his heart, and the tears would well up in her eyes. That's all—and it was everything.

10. Meditate on the following:

> *Singing cheerful songs to a person whose heart is heavy is as bad as stealing someone's jacket in cold weather or rubbing salt in a wound.*

Proverbs 25:20 (NLT)

A. What would be an example of "singing a cheerful song to a person whose heart is heavy?"

B. What two comparisons are made and what is the point?

C. Imagine you are with a friend who has just had a miscarriage. How would you apply the above proverb?

11. What does Romans 12:15 tell us about approaching the grieving person? Have you ever had someone approach you this way? If so, share something about it and how it made you feel.

12. To what does Proverbs 20:5 compare a person's heart? What can a "friend of understanding" do?

Grief counselors advise "empathetic listening." You don't offer solutions, but you repeat what the person had said, to make sure you really are listening and to show you truly hear her. Ask questions to better understand what she has said or have her elaborate. You may ask how she is dealing with the pain and mess in her life. When I have had an empathetic listener draw me out, I not only feel like she cares, but the deep waters of my soul are drawn into the healing light, and I understand myself better. Sometimes I don't know what I think until I see what I say, and so having a friend urging me to articulate my thoughts brings understanding, not only to her, but also to my own heart.

Action Assignment

Ask God to show you a hurting person to whom you might minister. Either talk to her when your paths cross naturally, or make a short visit. Listen empathetically. Apply what you have learned. Do this before you meet to discuss this week's lesson with your group. Pray and plan now, realizing that God may alter it.

The psalmist often prays against Israel's enemies. And we need to pray against our spiritual enemies, who do "smear us with lies," for Satan is the father of lies, and lies are his native language. Pray through Psalm 119:69-72 for strength in temptation and affliction.

Though the arrogant have smeared me with lies,
   I keep your precepts with all my heart.

Their hearts are callous and unfeeling,
   but I delight in your law.

It was good for me to be afflicted
   so that I might learn your decrees.

The law from your mouth is more precious to me
   than thousands of pieces of silver and gold.

DAY 4

The Multiplied Burden of Grief and Shame

We cannot know for certain if Naomi felt shame as well as grief, but she may have. Their choice to move to Moab was not, many commentators feel, a godly choice. She may have also known that her sons disobeyed the Lord in marrying unbelieving Moabite women. Her words, "My God has dealt severely with me," imply that she felt this was God's judgment, but she was burdened by the severity of His response. Naomi may have been innocent in all of this, affected by the choices of her husband and sons. John Donne wrote, "No man is an island." We affect each other by our choices.

When our family members fail, we can feel shame. Shame is Satan's technique; whereas, guilt is from the Holy Spirit. With shame, there is a general feeling of unworthiness, but no specific sin to repent of. With guilt, the conviction is specific, and repentance is possible.

When a sister feels not only grief, but shame, our silence adds to her feeling of being accused. There isn't one of us who couldn't be in her shoes, and we need to let her know that. Sharon, a godly woman whose son has just been given a prison sentence, hugged me hard when I said, "I hear you're going through a rough time."

She said, "Oh, Dee, most people don't say anything."

Ruth is my model. She doesn't criticize Naomi or quote Scripture. She stands by her side. She loves her. She shows Naomi she is still a woman of worth and that her God can still be trusted.

When my husband and I had a son who was a prodigal, it was harder to talk about our pain than if our son had simply been struggling with an illness. Whether it was true or not, we felt that part of our son's rebellion was due to our failure to parent wisely. Again, the women who ministered the most to me during that time were women who wept with me, assured me of their love and prayers, and let me know that they were confident that it would be okay in the end because God was faithful. It was to those women whom I could freely ask—can you see a behavior of which I should repent? Our son did turn around dramatically, and I am *so thankful* for the heartfelt prayers of my sister in Christ and for my son's repentant spirit.

When a woman loses a husband to death, the Christian community is better at coming alongside than when she loses a husband to divorce. Sometimes the Christian community will increase her pain. I just read an article in a Christian publication I respect, but it made me so angry. It piously stated: "In separation and divorce there is rarely, if ever, a case where one party is beyond reproach and the other should receive total blame." Of course there is always sin on both sides, for we are all sinners. But I wish this writer could know some of the women I have known well who have been victims of abuse. When they separate and demand their husbands get help for addiction and abuse, they are shamed by the Christian community. There are definitely cases where one party is a victim, and the sin lies primarily on the part of the perpetrator. These victims need, not shame, but support. We'll look at an example from Malachi that will equip you to help your sisters who are victims of abuse.

80

God calls husbands to protect their wives. That protection involves providing for them not only materially, but also emotionally, by being gentle, faithful, and sacrificial. He calls wives to honor and submit to their husbands. If a man does not provide for his family, 1 Timothy 5:8 says "he has denied the faith and is worse than an unbeliever." The picture Scripture gives is that a man is to "cover" his wife, as the Lord "covers" each of His children. Ruth goes to Boaz and asks him to "cover" her with his garment or skirt, meaning to protect and provide for her as a husband. The word translated garment is the Hebrew word *kanaph*.

13. How is the Hebrew word *kanaph* translated in the following psalm? What concept do you see?

> *He will cover you with his feathers, and under his wings you will find refuge;*
> *his faithfulness will be your shield and rampart.*

Psalm 91:4

14. How is *kanaph* translated in this passage from Ruth? What was Ruth asking Boaz to do? What would have his "covering" her meant?

> *When Boaz had finished eating and drinking and was in good spirits, he went over to lie down at the far end of the grain pile. Ruth approached quietly, uncovered his feet and lay down. In the middle of the night something startled the man, and he turned and discovered a woman lying at his feet.*
>
> *"Who are you?" he asked.*
>
> *"I am your servant Ruth," she said. "Spread the corner of your garment over me, since you are a kinsman-redeemer."*

If Boaz had refused Ruth's request, it would have been a dishonor to him for he was part of her covenant family and had a responsibility to her. However, there was an even "nearer" kinsman who was first in line and had a greater responsibility. Boaz, for legal reasons, must approach him first. The "nearer" kinsman refuses to "cover" Ruth for he fears that she will bear a son who will grow up and inherit the land from him. When he refuses, there is a ceremony to show his disgrace for not providing for his family.

15. Describe the ceremony that a "kinsman-redeemer" who refuses to redeem, protect, and provide must go through according to Deuteronomy 25:5-10.

Note the spitting in the face! There is a deeper symbolism here. When we become part of God's covenant family and join a local church (to refuse is irresponsible), we take on a God-given responsibility to our brothers and sisters in Christ. We are to care for, protect, and show God's grace to them. They are family. A refusal, for selfish reasons, is a disgrace to God and to the covenant family.

16. What refusal does the nearer kinsman make? How can you see he doesn't care for Ruth?

17. Describe the ceremony of disgrace in Ruth 4:1-8.

18. Read Malachi 2:10-17.

   A. What has "Judah" (another name for God's people) profaned? (v. 10)

   B. What specific sin have the men committed? (v. 11)

   C. What arrogant act have they heaped upon this sin? (vs. 12-13)

   D. Why is God angry with these men? Find as many reasons as you can in verses 14 and 15.

   E. What statement does God make to summarize His anger at these men in verse 16?

   Knowing that God is angry with an unfaithful spouse can help the faithful spouse to forgive, for she (or he) knows God will deal with him (or her).

   F. To whom was God addressing the statement "I hate divorce"? Why?

Sometimes the phrase "I hate divorce" is taken out of context and applied by believers to the victim. This is an example of shame. There are many victims who have no control over their spouse walking out with a new partner. Telling them that God hates divorce heaps shame upon betrayal. What they need is love and empathy. It is also true that women who are married to an abusive partner need support to separate. Often the only thing that will bring an abuser or someone in the bondage of addiction to his (or her) senses is separation.

19. How might you apply today's lesson to hurting sisters in your life?

Pray through Psalm 119:73-80 verbatim, but with your whole heart.

Your hands made me and formed me;
    give me understanding to learn your commands.

May those who fear you rejoice when they see me,
    for I have put my hope in your word.

I know, O LORD, that your laws are righteous,
    and in faithfulness you have afflicted me.

May your unfailing love be my comfort,
    according to your promise to your servant.

Let your compassion come to me that I may live,
    for your law is my delight.

May the arrogant be put to shame for wronging me without cause;
    but I will meditate on your precepts.

May those who fear you turn to me,
    those who understand your statutes.

May my heart be blameless toward your decrees,
    that I may not be put to shame.

DAY 5

· ·

When Confrontation Is Appropriate

The person in grief doesn't need solutions or confrontation, but rather your empathizing presence. But there are times when we must speak up. If we make the mistake of quietly empathizing when we should be alerting our friend to danger, we may actually be holding her hand as she walks toward the cliff. I was convicted by an observation Christian counselor Jay Adams makes in *Competent to Counsel*. He says that too often when a friend makes a comment like, "I guess I haven't been much of a mother or a wife," we respond by minimizing her confession. We'll say, "Don't talk like that, Susie; you know you haven't been that bad." I've done this— even if I know Susie is a terrible wife or mother! This is a destructive use of my feminine gift for empathy.

Adams says it would be much more productive to say, "Well now, that's a serious matter before God; how have you failed as a wife?" If we are close to someone who is considering divorce for unscriptural reasons: an abortion, marriage to an unbeliever, or anything that is clearly sin, we have a responsibility to speak the truth in love. Galatians 6:1 tells us, "Brothers, if someone is caught in a sin, you who are spiritual should restore him gently." How can you confront gently? By helping her discover how this choice may very well bring great pain into her life.

20. If you read chapter 6 of *The Friendships of Women*, did anything stand out to you? If so, what?

21. What does Proverbs 27:6 say? What does this mean?

22. Imagine that you are considering having an affair or an abortion, thinking this is something you truly want. What friends would you most likely listen to? What approach do you think might be effective? What would not be?

23. Were you able to empathize with a friend this week? If so, how? (Action Assignment)

24. Has this week's study impressed anything particular on you that could lead to a personal prayer request? Write down a sentence concerning that request or another personal need that you would be willing to lift up in prayer.

PRAYER TIME

Cluster in groups of three or four. Have each woman lift up her answer to question 23 in prayer, and then allow the others to support her. When there is a pause, another woman should lift up her need.

Seven

The Risk of Love

Intimacy is risky. No doubt about it. If I reach out to a woman to whom I am drawn, she may reject me. If I tell a woman that I love her, that I cherish her as a friend, she may respond little (or not at all). If I open my soul to another, trusting her with my dark side of failure, she may draw back in shocked silence (or she may tell others). Risky. Risky. Risky.

Then why do it? Why set ourselves up for hurt? Why not play it safe, as most men do? Because daring to take risks, as Ruth did, ignites the flame for bonding. In Sunday school many of us were told, "Dare to be a Daniel!" Perhaps we should be telling girls, "Risk being a Ruth!"

DAY I
. . . .

Risk Reaching Out

There was a time when a newcomer to the neighborhood was heralded as a joyous event. Those nearby embraced them with visits, gifts of food, and genuine interest. Not so today. When we moved from Seattle to a suburb of Portland, Oregon, I felt the anxiety of being separated from my women friends. It didn't help that it rained—steadily—for the first three weeks. (I was beginning to have great empathy for Noah!) No cheery neighbor braved the rain with a plateful of chocolate chip cookies. The gloom outside my window augmented the gloom in my spirit. If I wanted a friend, I was going to have to take the initiative. I began to plead unrelentingly with the Lord for a local sister in Christ who could be my friend. (And I have found that when my prayers are in earnest, then I am much more alert for the Lord's response.)

Knowing that group Bible study is usually a good source for friends, I decided to try Bible Study Fellowship, a national interdenominational organization. Portland's group happened to be meeting in a large church in our suburb. One Tuesday morning I drove up to the church in a downpour. I was astounded by the number of cars. Every space in the huge parking lot was taken, as were any available spaces on the streets near the church.

I parked three blocks away and ran sloshing through the puddles, trying to hurry while avoiding the earthworms that had crawled out for air. I walked through the double doors to hear the singing already in progress, acutely aware that I was late. The sanctuary was packed to overflowing with women. Somehow the camaraderie of the crowd made me feel lonelier than ever. I was going to slip into one of the chairs set up at the back for late-comers when a beautiful woman in the center section, front pew, caught my eye. She had the clean look that blondes without bangs have, her long, platinum hair pulled back in a neat, thick braid. Why do I feel so drawn to her? I wondered. Is it simply because she is so attractive? Or is it possible that the Holy Spirit is drawing my attention to her? Is she the friend for whom I've been praying? If God was leading me, I was going to have to walk in my wet and bedraggled state in front of everyone in order to sit next to her. All the way across. Risky. Maybe crazy. But so intense was my need for a friend that I did it.

She looked up from her hymnal, startled by my presence. (She looked so sophisticated—so dry!) But she smiled reassuringly, moved over to give me room, and shared her hymnal. I felt hopeful until the singing and the lecture ended and she left, without a word, to go to her small group. I stayed with a handful of newcomers to get my instructions. We filled out some forms and then were dismissed early, being told we would be assigned to regular small groups the next week. No one spoke to me personally. I went home, feeling lonelier than before I came.

I did risk going back, however. I didn't see the tall, cool blonde until we divided into our small groups. I was assigned to room 101, the room for those whose last names began with letters *Br* through *Ca*. When I walked in, I was surprised to see her, seated at a round table with nine other women. (I wondered, Providence or coincidence?) Her name was Pam Carlson. When she saw me, her face didn't register recognition. (I do look different, however, when I'm not dripping wet.) Reserved, Pam spoke only once during the whole hour, but then with an earnestness and insightfulness that stilled the room. She was an intent listener, leaning forward in her chair, making eye contact with whomever was speaking. There are so few good listeners, I thought, and remembered how C. S. Lewis in *Mere Christianity* had said that listening might be one of the first things you notice in a genuine believer. Most people are so caught up in themselves that they are not good listeners—but Jesus can change that. At one point, when a description of the crucifixion was read from Scripture, Pam's eyes filled with tears. I felt coldhearted in comparison. Pam hadn't lost her first love. Again, I felt drawn to her. Again, I determined to risk reaching out to her.

After the study, Pam swept up her books and darted out the door. Determined, I charged after her. I fell into step with her in the church parking lot. I told her I appreciated the comment she'd made. (I was hoping she'd realize this was an overture of friendship.) But instead our conversation took a nosedive as she said, "Thank you! See you next week!" and ran toward her car, leaving me standing alone, slightly embarrassed.

I chastised myself: "You're behaving foolishly. God is not leading, and Pam is not interested in being your friend." I decided to abandon my wild goose chase while I still had dignity. (Had I been familiar with Ruth's persistence in the face of rejection, I might have been stronger.) But just as I was about to give up, God intervened.

Steve and I had tried four different churches during our first month in Oregon. None of them seemed right. That Sunday we decided to visit a small church in the country. When we walked in the door, Pam saw me before I saw her. She and her husband were the official greeters. "Dee!" she called out to me. I turned, surprised that anyone would know my name. When I saw her, I had the sensation you have when you realize the pieces are fitting together and God is answering prayer.

Encouraged, I asked Pam if she could come over for coffee the next day.

She smiled warmly and said, "I'd love to!"

WARMUP

What stands out to you from the above story? Can you identify with it in any way? If so, how?

1. Read through the four short chapters in Ruth carefully. Write RISK in the margin whenever you see Ruth taking a risk.

   A. What risks did you see Ruth taking? Which ones do you think were based on faith and why?

   B. How did God bless her for her risks?

   C. What happened with her friendship with Naomi as a result?

   D. What happened with her friendship with the women of Bethlehem as a result?

   E. What was her reputation, according to Ruth 3:11?

   F. What happened with her friendship with Boaz?

2. What could you learn from Ruth about reaching out in friendship that you could apply to your life?

Ruth's risks, based on faith, were an enormous blessing to Naomi. Ruth continued risking, even when there was no response from Naomi, who seems, in her grief, like the frozen ground of winter. Eventually Ruth sees a tiny green blade poke up from the snow, and then stand tall, and finally, burst into fullness, bearing fruit. Naomi is restored. The following octrain from Psalm 119 is one I can imagine Naomi praying. If you are not feeling this way now, pray responsively for someone who might be.

My soul faints with longing for your salvation,
*   but I have put my hope in your word.*

My eyes fail, looking for your promise;
*   I say, "When will you comfort me?"*

Though I am like a wineskin in the smoke,
*   I do not forget your decrees.*

How long must your servant wait?
*   When will you punish my persecutors?*

The arrogant dig pitfalls for me,
*   contrary to your law.*

All your commands are trustworthy;
*   help me, for men persecute me without cause.*

They almost wiped me from the earth,
*   but I have not forsaken your precepts.*

Preserve my life according to your love,
*   and I will obey the statutes of your mouth.*

Psalm 119:81-88

DAY 2

Risk Vulnerability

With kindred spirits, with a friendship given to you by God, it is possible to jump in at the "middle of a friendship." You can begin with personal issues right away. Before I had even poured coffee for Pam, she asked me, "How did you come to Christ?" She was an active listener, prodding me with questions. Then it was my turn to prod, and I heard how God had wooed her to a Billy Graham Crusade, which she thought she was going to "on a lark."

Pam risked opening herself up to me, telling me of her struggle to live simply. "I love nice things—and they have a giant grip on my mind and heart." We talked about how we thought a Christian should live if he's not being squeezed into the world's mold. Then Pam broke the intensity of our discussion and sent us into gales of laughter by commenting, "I'm so glad I got my antiques before I was saved!"

Pam and I were finishing the other's sentences, eager to press on to the height of our thoughts. Author Randolph Bourne said, "One comes from friends ... with a high sense of elation and the brimming adequacy of life ... the keen thoughts, the trains of arguments, the pregnant thoughts that spring so spontaneously to mind."

Walter Wangerin, author of *The Book of the Dun Cow*, told Margaret Smith, "You like to jump into a friendship and not start at the beginning but in the middle." She said, "That's exactly right!" And I agree. Who wants to go through the boring preliminaries? If I can avoid them, I will!

It's not wise to bear your soul to everyone. But if you sense someone has been given to you by God, you can take small risks initially by telling them some deeper truths about yourself. And as someone has shown themselves to be trustworthy, be willing to let them see the more private, even the less beautiful parts of your heart. C. S. Lewis wrote, "Eros will have naked bodies; friendship naked personalities." Our lack of inhibition in making ourselves vulnerable is one of the main reasons, I am convinced, that women have real friends. Ruth and Naomi might have stayed on an "in-law" basis had Ruth held Naomi at arm's length. But she never did. When asked about her night with Boaz, Ruth told her mother-in-law everything!

Vulnerability hastens bonding. Charlotte explained it like this: "When a woman friend confides in me, I feel honored, esteemed that she would trust me so."

3. Be a detective (asking what, who, why, how...) as you look, in this case, at Ruth and Boaz and how they each took risks in vulnerability. What was said, by whom and to whom, and do you think it felt risky for them? If so, why?

   A. Ruth 2:8-9

   B. Ruth 2:10

   C. Ruth 2:11-12

Notice how Boaz prays "on the spot," as he did in Ruth 2:4. How good it would be if we could get in this habit. Too often we promise to pray and forget.

   D. Ruth 2:13

   E. Ruth 2:14

   F. Ruth 2:15-16

Often pride keeps us from sharing how we truly feel, from saying the affirming thoughts or questions that come to our mind. But worshipers of God, who find their security in Him, are often released from the prison bars of fear, jealousy, or pride that keep many from sharing freely.

4. Be a detective again with David and Jonathan. Who says what to whom? How do you see vulnerability? If you see a result, comment.

   A. 1 Samuel 18:1-4

   B. 1 Samuel 20:41-42

5. Again, what do you see with Mary and Elizabeth in Luke 1:41-45?

6. In this Bible study group, how could you apply what you have learned today?

7. In friendships given to you by God, how could you apply what you have learned today?

Pray through Psalm 119:89-92 verbatim, but with your heart and mind.

Your word, O LORD, is eternal;
   it stands firm in the heavens.

Your faithfulness continues through all generations;
   you established the earth, and it endures.

Your laws endure to this day,
   for all things serve you.

If your law had not been my delight,
   I would have perished in my affliction.

DAY 3

Flattery Versus Affirmation

Why is it that we so often hold back the affirming word? Perhaps we fear we are flattering. We shouldn't flatter—for flattery is a technique of the wicked, and its end is destruction. But we should affirm. Today, we'll look at the difference between flattery and affirmation. Then, tomorrow, we'll look at models from Ruth who used affirmation well.

Pray through Psalm 119:93-96 to prepare your heart for study.

I will never forget your precepts,
**   for by them you have preserved my life.**

Save me, for I am yours;
**   I have sought out your precepts.**

The wicked are waiting to destroy me,
**   but I will ponder your statutes.**

To all perfection I see a limit;
**   but your commands are boundless.**

8. Write down everything you can learn about flattery from the following:

    A. Psalm 12:2-3

    B. Psalm 36:1-2

    C. Psalm 55:21

    D. 1 Thessalonians 2:3-6

9. How would you define flattery, based on what you've learned from the above Scriptures?

10. Meditate on Proverbs 26:23-28.

    [23] *Like a coating of glaze over earthenware are fervent lips with an evil heart.*

    A. In the above, what word picture is given? What is the point of this comparison?

²⁴ A malicious man disguises himself with his lips, but in his heart he harbors deceit.

B. In the above, what is the disguise, and what is being disguised?

²⁵ Though his speech is charming, do not believe him, for seven abominations fill his heart.

C. "Seven" is a way of saying "complete" in Scripture. What does this tell you?

²⁶ His malice may be concealed by deception, but his wickedness will be exposed in the assembly.
²⁷ If a man digs a pit, he will fall into it; if a man rolls a stone, it will roll back on him.

D. What is the end of the flatterer?

²⁸ A lying tongue hates those it hurts, and a flattering mouth works ruin.

E. Why is it important to discern both lies and flattery?

11. What do you learn about encouragement or "good words" from the following?
    A. Proverbs 12:25

    B. Proverbs 15:23

    C. Proverbs 16:24

    D. Proverbs 25:11

12. How would you describe the difference between flattery and encouragement or affirmation based on what you have learned today?

DAY 4

Risk Affirming Others

This life is hard, the enemy is real, and very few make the effort to say the encouraging word. But oh, what a difference it can make. We are so often like flailing kites, but an encouraging word is like a good stiff breeze that can send our kites soaring. If our motive is not to get something from someone, but instead, to speak the truth that we truly do feel in our hearts, then we are encouraging, not flattering. It's easier to say nothing—we may think the person doesn't need to hear it—but let us begin with this question:

13. How welcome are words of encouragement to you? Do you wish you heard them more or less? Why?

The book of Ruth is filled with words of encouragement and heartfelt prayers. It is a beautiful portrait of covenant people taking the risk of saying the affirming word or prayer that is in their hearts. Today we will see how easily they pray (on the spot—which is a great model because then you do not forget to do it), how easily they affirm. Usually the affirmation is not about externals, but about character. Sometimes the affirmation comes in the form of a prayer, but it is not flattery, for it is from the heart. What a model for us!

14. In each of the following, discover: Who was encouraging? Who was being encouraged? Was it a prayer as well? What did they say, and what did they mean? What response can you see? Find everything you can, for it truly will give you light for being a good friend. (To get you started, the first is answered.)

    A. Ruth 1:8-9—Naomi is affirming her two daughters-in-law through prayer. She tells them they have been good daughters-in-law and good wives by saying, "May the LORD show kindness to you, as you have shown to your dead and to me." She prays they will find "rest" in the home of a husband. Here she is praying they will find a kind man and have a good marriage. She is praying they will be blessed as they have blessed. We know that her prayer was answered for Ruth through Boaz. We do not know what happened to Orpah, for she faded out of the pages of Scripture when she turned back to Moab.

    B. Ruth 1:9-10—Can affirmation include more than words? If so, what?

    C. Ruth 1:14

    D. Ruth 1:16-18

E. Ruth 2:4a (First part of verse)

F. Ruth 2:4b (Second part of verse)

G. Ruth 2:6-7

H. Ruth 2:8-9

15. In an earlier lesson we looked at this next section as an example of "woman talk," or "rapport talk," where they take one another to greater heights. This time look at it as a model of encouragement, for much of their encouragement has to do with how they are telling one another that they see God at work. Find whatever you can.

A. Read Ruth 2:20.

Naomi said to her daughter-in-law, "May he be blessed of the LORD who has not withdrawn his kindness to the living and to the dead." Again Naomi said to her, "The man is our relative, he is one of our closest relatives."

Ruth 2:20 (NAS)

B. Ruth 2:21

C. Ruth 2:22

D. Ruth 3:1-4

E. Ruth 3:5

John Macarthur, in *Twelve Extraordinary Women*, says that "Even to enlightened twenty-first century minds," Naomi's plan "seems surprisingly plucky." Naomi is basically asking Ruth to take her place as the one to receive the blessing from the kinsman-redeemer and to propose to Boaz! Ruth really couldn't know how Boaz would respond. But she trusted her mother-in-law, trusted her mother-in-law's God, and was willing to take this risk.

16. There is tenderness in this scene between Ruth and Boaz. Consider how Ruth's bold act must have encouraged Boaz and how Boaz's words must have encouraged Ruth.

    A. Ruth 3:8-9

    B. Ruth 3:10-11

17. Note how often character traits are affirmed! Boaz said, "All my fellow townsmen know you are a woman of excellence." Consider what that must have meant to this Moabite woman who was ashamed of her past. What do you think it means to be "a woman of excellence?"

18. Look closely at the prayer/affirmation from the women of Bethlehem in Ruth 4:14-15. Write down everything you see.

DAY 5

Telling the Truth about Ourselves

Telling the truth about ourselves not only hastens bonding, it can embolden a hurting person to open a festering wound that needs to be opened. A godly woman told me, "Sometimes, when I am aware that it would be helpful to a friend to open up to me about a problem, but sense hesitancy, I'll lead the way by making myself vulnerable. I'll share where I am hurting or failing."

And we are all hurting. This life is full of pain. We are all failing in some ways. Our sin nature is strong and rears its ugly head in the best of us. We need each other's fervent prayers. We need to be honest with each other in our prayer times, and when another risks being truly honest, we need to treat her "confession" with the same care as if she had asked us to keep an heirloom safe for her. We don't treat it carelessly, but wrap it up, put it in a safe place, and realize we have been given the honor of being trusted.

19. In what areas are you truly hurting? In what areas are you failing? Write these down and ask the Lord to show you whom you could trust with this confession.

Make this your common practice: Confess your sins to each other and pray for each other so that you can live together whole and healed. The prayer of a person living right with God is something powerful to be reckoned with.

James 5:16 *(MSG)*

If you are reading *The Friendships of Women*, what stood out to you from chapter 7?

PRAYER TIME

Cluster in groups of three. Begin by affirming each other—what are some things you are thankful for in the other two? Then thank God in prayer and lift up your requests to Him.

Eight

Best Friends

Each time my husband and I moved, I was restless until I found a woman who could be the kind of friend for which Anne of Green Gables longed when she said: "I've dreamed of meeting her all my life ... a bosom friend—an intimate friend, you know—a really kindred spirit to whom I can confide my inmost soul."

Though my husband was my dearest friend, I had a longing for a special woman friend with whom I could confide, connect, and console. Best friendships reflect, most clearly, the gold in the friendships of women—but also the dross. I would give my very life for a best friend, but I could also become as petulant as a jilted lover when a soul mate withdrew for a season. Lillian Rubin says, "Best friends have the power to help and to hurt in ways that no one but a mate or a lover can match."

Both Ruth/Naomi and Mary/Elizabeth had inter-generational friendships between relatives. We really don't have a strong example of "best" female friends in Scripture between peers who were not related. We do, however, have one of men. And David and Jonathan, perhaps because they were two rare right-brained males, can teach even women a few things about friendship.

DAY I

What Is a Best Friend, a Soul Mate?

When I talked to women and asked them if they had a best friend, some would say, "I have two best friends," or, "I have three best friends." When I objected, saying that seemed to contradict the word *best*, they persisted. I came to realize that while *best friend* often does mean the friend you love the most, it can also mean a friend with whom you have a deep rapport and would consider a soul mate, a kindred spirit. There is a special bond that sets friends like these apart from the rest, and though they are very rare, you may be blessed with more than one. In fact, considering the feminine tendency toward dependency, it would be healthy to seek more than one soul mate and to give our closest friends freedom to do the same.

Aristotle expressed the concept of soul mates when he said, "Friendship is a single soul living in two bodies." Bets said of her friendship with Beth: "There is not another person in the world who knows the things about me that Beth knows. She knows me inside and out. It's something spiritual, something in our souls—we are to each other like second selves."

Studies show that men, in sharp contrast to women, are not likely to be able to name a best friend. In her research, Lillian Rubin found that men shrugged off her questions about best friends: "Best friends are for kids." One man, piqued, said, "Only a woman would have so **** many questions about friends and make it so important." How interesting, therefore, that the very best friends in Scripture are two men!

WARMUP

How would you define a "best friend," a "soul mate"?

1. On the basis of 1 Samuel 18:1, how would you define a soul mate?

Their friendship is unusual, surpassing even the friendships of most women. Some have accused David and Jonathan of practicing homosexuality. But if that were so, then the Lord, who clearly defines the practice of homosexuality as sin, couldn't have said what He did about David: "For David had done what was right in the eyes of the LORD and had not failed to keep any of the LORD's commands all the days of his life—except in the case of Uriah the Hittite" (1 Kings 15:5). I believe the reason many men are uncomfortable with David and Jonathan is that they have never experienced this kind of friendship, except perhaps with a woman with whom they are also sexually one. In the case of David and Jonathan, we are told "the soul of Jonathan was knit with the soul of David." It was their souls, not their bodies, which were knit together.

2. The same Hebrew word which is translated "knit" in 1 Samuel 18:1 is used in the story of Joseph's brothers pleading with the ruler of Egypt to leave their youngest brother, Benjamin, with their father. (They do not realize they are pleading with Joseph, whom they had sold into slavery years before.) Read the context in Genesis 22:19-31. Then define, as best as you can, the meaning and emotion in this phrase "bound up" or "knit" as it is used in Genesis 44:30. What light does this throw on 1 Samuel 18:1?

3. Read the following passages and see if you can find any parallels between David and Jonathan that might have caused their souls to be knit together.

JONATHAN	DAVID
A. 1 Samuel 14:6-15	1 Samuel 17:4-37
B. 1 Samuel 20:30-33	1 Samuel 17:28

I suspect that David and Jonathan were rare right-brained males. Both were extremely accurate marksmen (David with his slingshot, Jonathan with his bow) and this, scientists now suspect, is one indication of a dominant right hemisphere. (There's an interesting passage in Judg. 20:16 that tells of "seven hundred chosen men who were left-handed, each of whom could sling a stone at a hair and not miss.") David was a poet, a psalmist, a harpist—all gifts that we would attribute to the creative right hemisphere. And, as we will see, Jonathan was certainly able to express his feelings, which is also a strength of the right hemisphere. This may be, in part, why their friendship was so deep—for right-brained males can teach even women a few things about friendship!

4. Is there someone to whom your soul is knit? Perhaps more than one? Who? How would you describe this relationship?

DAY 2

Being Drawn to Saints and Poets

What drew Jonathan to David? Surely he was impressed with the fact that David, alone among the Israelites, had the courage to take on the giant that was defaming God's name. I, too, am drawn to those who are willing to take on the giants in our world of injustice, hunger, loneliness, and more. When I saw Lorma take on the giant of hunger by setting up her shop to sell things made by craftsmen in third-world countries, I wanted to be Lorma's friend. When Janet took on the giant of loneliness by inviting international students into her home weekly, I was drawn. Giant slayers won't be sitting back on the sidelines. Seeking God's wisdom, they plan well, and act, in faith, to carry it out.

Jonathan no doubt also recognized the poet in David as he listened to David play and sing the psalms to his father, Saul.

I played the role of Emily in our high school's presentation of Thornton Wilder's *Our Town*. One scene lingers in my memory. After Emily has died, she is allowed to watch her loved ones on earth. She is poignantly aware that they are scurrying about, taking life for granted, just as she did. With tears in her eyes, Emily watches her mama and remembers the little things, like "sunflowers, coffee, new-ironed dresses and hot baths." She cries, "Oh, earth, you're too wonderful for anybody to realize you." Then she turns and asks the stage manager, "Do any human beings ever realize life while they live it?—every, every minute?" And he answers, "No. The saints and poets, maybe—they do, some."

Poets and saints see things other people miss. If we look carefully, most of us can find people who have poets' imaginations, who stretch us because their thoughts and their lifestyles have not been squeezed into the world's mold. We can also find "saints" who are so abiding in Christ and His Word that they see life differently from most Christians. Jesus says the mouth speaks what the heart is full of, and with some people, it is like sitting under a spiritual fountain, being sprinkled with the overflow of a rich heart. Poets are reflective, looking at life and seeing, asking thoughtful questions, drawing you out because they really care about how you think and feel. They take the road less traveled: They may be living simply, reading the classics, or dedicated to prayer.

This year I'm participating in a reading group at our church led by a saintly man who is also a philosophy professor at the University of Nebraska. The first day of Ethics, he asks his class: "How do you decide what's right and what's wrong?"

One after one, they say, in various ways: "Whatever I think is right is right."

The next day, the wise professor comes in, sits on his desk, scratches his beard, and says, "I'm going to grade differently than the way it is stated in the syllabus. I'm going to do what I think is right. I'm going to grade you on the basis of whether I like you or not. Bribes will work. I also like people who drive nice cars..."

The class starts buzzing. This isn't fair! But, he said, "It's what I think. So, it's right." With a twinkle in his eye, he tells me, later: "We'll see how many are really social relativists."

So, when I heard this professor was leading a reading group, I knew I wanted to be there. We're going slowly through *The Chronicles of Narnia* this year. The vision of C. S. Lewis, aided by this local "saint and poet" is helping me see so much more, and that influences the way I am looking at life on a daily basis.

David was a giant slayer, a saint, and a poet. It's one of the reasons godly individuals throughout Christendom have been strengthened by praying the Psalms, many of which were authored by David. We pray better when we have that help than we do just praying our own thoughts. Begin, today, by praying responsively through Psalm 119:97-104. You may not have the same love of God's Word that the psalmist did, but you can ask for it.

Oh, how I love your law!
I meditate on it all day long.

Your commands make me wiser than my enemies,
for they are ever with me.

I have more insight than all my teachers,
for I meditate on your statutes.

I have more understanding than the elders,
for I obey your precepts.

*I have kept my feet from every evil path
    so that I might obey your word.*

*I have not departed from your laws,
    for you yourself have taught me.*

*How sweet are your words to my taste,
    sweeter than honey to my mouth!*

*I gain understanding from your precepts;
    therefore I hate every wrong path.*

5. The Philistines have been defaming God's name and causing God's people grief from the time Jonathan was a boy. What kind of grief were they causing in each of the following passages?

    1 Samuel 13:5-7

    1 Samuel 13:19-22

6. How had Jonathan, himself, seen God go with him when he fought against the Philistines in 1 Samuel 14:1-14?

7. Just before the famous greeting scene, in which the soul of Jonathan is knit to the soul of David, and Jonathan commits himself to David, David slays Goliath. What, according to 1 Samuel 17:57, is David holding? How is this significant concerning cementing the friendship between David and Jonathan?

All this fighting may seem bloody and irrelevant to us, particularly as women. But it is important to realize that the battles in the Old Testament are a picture of the spiritual battles we face every day. When David prays, in the Psalms, against his enemies, we can apply this by praying against our spiritual enemies.

8. With whom do we wrestle, according to Ephesians 6:32?

Not only was David a giant slayer, he was a poet. Another fascinating scene between David and Saul, which Jonathan probably witnessed, occurs in 1 Samuel 16. David, though just a lad, has just been anointed by the prophet Samuel to be the future king of Israel. Saul has been a disobedient king, and God is removing His hand from Saul. Not only that, God sends a distressing spirit to Saul.

9. Read 1 Samuel 16:14-23 and describe what happens to Saul and how his distress is alleviated.

10. Why do you think that David's playing alleviated the distressing spirit? See 2 Chronicles 20:21-22.

11. As you consider all of the above, why do you think the heart of Jonathan was so strongly drawn to the heart of David?

12. What application could you make to your life?

DAY 3
....

Don't Let Your Closest Friends Be Weak Sisters

Recently a bright and enthusiastic woman at one of my retreats came up to me and said, "I want to tell you I read *The Friendships of Women* fifteen years ago and it changed my life. Not only was I delivered from homosexuality, but there were so many other things in that book that impacted me. Dee, I remember so many things." And then, bless her, she was specific, listing them, including, "I look for poets and giant slayers. I do! And it's made my friendships so rich."

A best friendship begins, often, with the same sort of feelings that lovers feel when meeting. We notice something and are pulled. It may be giant slaying, it may be poetic vision, or it may be something ineffable, but we are drawn.

We would be wise to consider what attracts us to a woman. When we are pulled to that which is lovely and Christlike, when we notice someone who is living a radically obedient life, then those are the best impulses to act on. This is when it is definitely worth taking a risk in reaching out to someone. We will become like our closest friends. One of the costliest mistakes we can make is to have a weak Christian for a best friend.

Meditate on the following.

I wrote you in my [previous] letter not to associate [closely and habitually] with unchaste (impure) people—

Not [meaning of course that you must] altogether shun the immoral people of this world, or the greedy graspers and cheats and thieves or idolaters, since otherwise you would need to get out of the world and human society altogether!

But now I write to you not to associate with anyone who bears the name of [Christian] brother if he is known to be guilty of immorality or greed, or is an idolater [whose soul is devoted to any object that usurps the place of God], or is a person with a foul tongue [railing, abusing, reviling, slandering], or is a drunkard or a swindler or a robber. [No] you must not so much as eat with such a person.

1 Corinthians 5:9-11 (AMP)

The above is in the context of Paul writing to the Corinthian church about church discipline. They have allowed a man who has been sexually immoral to remain as an active member. Paul is pleading with them, for the sake of their local church and for the sake of the man, to discipline him. But there is an application for us here in friendship as well.

13. Meditate on one of Jesus' final prayers for us in John 17:15. What didn't He pray for, according to this verse? What did He pray for?

14. How is this prayer paralleled in the 1 Corinthians 5:9-11 passage that you just read?

15. What warning is given in 1 Corinthians 5:9-11? Find as many things as you can about the person with whom you should not be close friends. Describe characteristics you might see in her life. Is she a Christian or not? Explain.

He (or she) calls himself a brother, and only God can see his heart. But the church can decide (yes, even "judge"), on the basis of behavior, to discipline him. Second Thessalonians 3:14-15 has similar counsel, yet also urges us not to treat him as an enemy, but to admonish him as a brother. Only God knows if he is truly a brother, and in the end, will separate the wheat from the tares.

16. What warning does 1 Corinthians 15:33 give?

17. What warning does 2 Corinthians 6:14 give?

The above warning in context, applies to a working relationship. An ox and a donkey do not plow well yoked together. They do not do the job well and bring harm to each other. This is the reason, for example, that my husband went into medical practice with other brothers in Christ. They agreed not to make the bottom line of their practice money, but ministry. However, this passage could certainly also be applied to the close relationships of marriage or best friendships. In these closest of relationships, we are to avoid being yoked with an unbeliever.

Having said this, it is also important not to live in a Christian cloister. God's Word exhorts us to go out into the world, befriending those who do not know Him, sharing Christ with them, and discipling them.

18. Are you befriending non-Christians? Are you being the love of Christ to them? Explain.

DAY 4

Seek Out Those Who Love the Lord Deeply

Not only are we to avoid being closely and habitually in contact with someone who calls herself a sister yet talks and walks like someone in the world does, we are also to seek for our closest friends, those who love the Lord deeply. This is another thread from God's friendship pattern.

When I look at the really good choices I made this week, so often they were influenced by a friend. Look, for example, at the last few days:

Friday: Traveling, stayed with Scharfs. Love the way they always read a psalm at breakfast and pray for a different country each day. I am reminded to be a world Christian, praying for countries. Their daughter-in-law talks about a book she has loved, *Girl Meets God*. I make a note to get it.

Saturday: Walk with my friend Beth and we pray for our kids. We have a good discussion on how better to speak the truth in love. She tells me I must read the new boundaries book—*Face to Face: Having That Difficult Conversation*. I order it from Barnes and Noble. Amazing. Now I'm giving it to others.

Sunday: Have lunch after church with Christy and Ellen. I tell them I've gained fifteen pounds since Steve's death—I'm turning to the false god of food for comfort, and I can't seem to stop. They pray for me on the spot. Then Ellen tells me about a free Bible study on a Web site called SettingCaptivesFree.com. There's one specifically for food called The Lord's Table. It helped her—she thinks it will help me. I check it out—am starting it—excited about it.

19. Look at the last couple of weeks of your life. In what ways have your closest friends helped you spiritually?

20. Consider what we can glean about the spiritual strength of the six individuals we are studying.

   A. How do you think Naomi differed from the women of Moab such that Ruth was drawn to her? What do you see in Naomi, even in her grief, that tells you something about her faith? How does she strengthen Ruth?

B. What do we know about Ruth, according to Ruth 3:11? What are some ways you see spiritual strength in Ruth? How does she strengthen Naomi?

C. What does Acts 13:22 tell us about David? What evidence do you see for this? How does he strengthen Jonathan?

D. What have you learned about Jonathan that exemplifies his heart for God? How does he strengthen David?

E. What do we know about Elizabeth from Luke 1:6? How else do you see her heart for God? How does she strengthen Mary?

F. What do we know about Mary from Luke 1:28 and Luke 1:38? How else do you see her heart for God? How does she strengthen Elizabeth?

21. As you look at your own life, would someone who loves the Lord deeply be drawn to you? Explain.

Pray responsively through Psalm 119:105-112.

Your word is a lamp to my feet
and a light for my path.

I have taken an oath and confirmed it,
that I will follow your righteous laws.

I have suffered much;
preserve my life, O Lord, according to your word.

Accept, O Lord, the willing praise of my mouth,
and teach me your laws.

Though I constantly take my life in my hands,

I will not forget your law.

The wicked have set a snare for me,
but I have not strayed from your precepts.

Your statutes are my heritage forever;
they are the joy of my heart.

My heart is set on keeping your decrees
to the very end.

DAY 5

Asking the Lord for Friends

My life is so much richer because the Lord has taught me to pray and look for certain kinds of friends for my closest friends. Friends like Ruth and Jonathan are gifts from God. Though we can't demand a gift, we can ask. James tells us we have not because we ask not. Then, be alert to how God might be leading.

Sometimes He will bring someone across your path. I realize now that there were times, especially when I was younger, that God may have brought someone across my path, but I didn't recognize her because, instead of looking for spiritual strength, I looked at the outward appearance of age, beauty, or clothing. There were also times I failed to take risks in reaching out to someone to whom I was drawn. She was there—but I missed her. There were also times I ran ahead of the Lord, because I was lonely, and chose someone who was not His best for me.

There are seasons when He chooses for you to walk alone, so that your trust is only in Him. This was true of Jesus when He walked the earth, so surely it will be true of us. Sometimes we ask Him for a strong friend, and He makes us wait. Naomi was surrounded by unbelievers when she moved to Moab, and they lived there ten years before Ruth makes her famous conversion statement. David and Jonathan each grew up in families that seemed, in many ways, weak spiritually. Elizabeth went into a three-month seclusion before the Lord brought Mary.

22. What do you learn about waiting on the Lord from the following?

    A. Psalm 123:1-2

    B. Isaiah 40:31

Jesus Himself often waited on His Father. He had twelve close friends (whom He chose prayerfully), and among those twelve, there were three who were even closer. Yet even they sometimes let Jesus down, and He had only His Father.

23. What can you learn from the model of Christ that might apply to friendship?
    A. Luke 6:12-13

    B. Luke 9:28

    C. Matthew 26:36-46

24. Many of David's psalms were written when he was alone, waiting on the Lord. Can we even imagine? Here he was the future king but hunted like a criminal, fleeing from cave to cave in the wilderness. This isn't quite the way he expected his life would be. Yet, again and again, He clings to the Lord, waiting. Consider Psalm 27. What are some phrases that stand out to you? What is David's closing conclusion?

25. Have there been times when you have had to wait on the Lord in friendship? What have you learned in those times?

26. Have you asked the Lord for strong Christian friends?

27. If you read chapter 8 of *The Friendships of Women*, what stood out to you?

PRAYER TIME

Cluster in groups of three or four. Have each woman lift up a need of her heart and then allow the others to support her. When there is a pause, another woman should lift up her need.

Nine

Unfailing Love

What we long for, Solomon tells us, is "unfailing love" (Prov. 19:22). I want friends who are like sisters—who will love me, be there when I need them, and give me grace when I let them down. Yet Solomon also tells us the "unfailing love" is very rare. *The Message* puts it like this:

Lots of people claim to be loyal and loving, but where on earth can you find one?

Proverbs 20:6 *(MSG)*

This week we'll look at the biblical concept of "unfailing love." What does it really mean? Can we actually hope for it from friends? And to whom should we be giving it? And how, considering our depravity, can we possibly love with unfailing love?

DAY I

Family Ties

When I was ten, I locked my sister's prom date in the fruit cellar. I thought it was a tremendous joke as I watched her steam increase over his tardiness. But though she may have wanted to, Sally didn't disown me. She's my sister, and blood ties rarely end.

My adolescent passage was torment for the family confined to my shelter. Mother said it was like living with someone who was going through three nonstop years of premenstrual tension: If she raised an eyebrow, it could release hysteria from me. But she held on and waited for this time to pass. She's my mother, and blood ties rarely end.

My sisters and I live in three different states: Texas, Utah, and Nebraska. We have not been geographically close since we left our childhood home. But we see each other at least annually, and we stay in touch almost daily by e-mail. We are not going to allow the mobility of our lives to keep us from being close. We are sisters, and blood ties rarely end.

Writer Lesley Dormen said that her family isn't going to cross her off their Christmas card list if she is impatient or crabby. She elaborates: If my mother and I exchange hurtful words, the incident has the power to pierce both of us to the heart. But I know with absolute certainty that neither my mother nor my brother will ever abandon me. We're bound to each other for good. We're family....

One study found that only 3 percent of siblings permanently disconnect. This is the power of blood. This is the power of family.

One of the ways God helps us to understand His love for us and the love He longs for us to have for each other is by using word pictures of family love. If you grew up in a truly dysfunctional home, these pictures may not be helpful to you. But if you grew up in a family that was even a bit healthy, then you have tasted God's love for us as our Father, and the love and support He longs for us to have as brothers and sisters.

WARMUP

Choose one example of a family member showing you tenderness. What did you see this in this person? If you didn't have any family members like this, choose an example of God showing you mercy and not giving up on you.

1. Read Psalm 103:13-14.

    A. To what does the psalmist compare God's love in verse 13?

    B. What are some ways a good father has compassion on his children?

    C. What does God know about us that is similar to a father's knowledge according to verse 14?

2. What thought is expressed in 1 John 3:1-2? What are some of the ramifications of this truth?

3. Read 1 Timothy 5:1-2 and describe how we are exhorted to treat individuals in the body of Christ. Explain what this means in each instance.

4. Exhortations often come in "family terms," appealing to us as brothers and sisters. In each of the following, define the exhortation and also the appeal to our tie as family members. You may need to look up the context if you don't remember the parable.

    A. From The Parable of the Unmerciful Servant:

"Shouldn't you have mercy on your fellow servant just as I had on you?" Then the angry king sent the man to prison until he had paid every penny.

"That's what my heavenly Father will do to you if you refuse to forgive your brothers and sisters in your heart."

Matthew 18:33-35 (NLT)

Exhortation?

Appeal to family ties?

B. From the story of the Prodigal Son:

"And he said to him, 'Son, you are always with me, and all that I have is yours. It was right that we should make merry and be glad, for your brother was dead and is alive again, and was lost and is found.'"

Luke 15:31-32 (NLT)

Exhortation?

Appeal to family ties?

C. From the story of Abraham and Lot:

So Abram said to Lot, "Let's not have any quarreling between you and me, or between your herdsmen and mine, for we are brothers. Is not the whole land before you? Let's part company. If you go to the left, I'll go to the right; if you go to the right, I'll go to the left."

Genesis 13:8-9

Exhortation?

Appeal to family ties?

D. What exhortation or appeal do all of the above three incidents have in common? How do you find this again in Psalm 133?

5. Are you at peace with your brothers and sisters in your covenant family? If not, is there any sin you could humbly confess to one who is estranged from you? Is there any way, in so far as it lies with you, to be at peace with him?

Close today by praying responsively through Psalm 119:114-120. Instead of thinking of it in terms of others, turn the light around on yourself. Is your walk as good as your talk?

You are my refuge and my shield;
I have put my hope in your word.

Away from me, you evildoers,
that I may keep the commands of my God!

Sustain me according to your promise, and I will live;
do not let my hopes be dashed.

Uphold me, and I will be delivered;
I will always have regard for your decrees.

You reject all who stray from your decrees,
for their deceitfulness is in vain.

All the wicked of the earth you discard like dross;
therefore I love your statutes.

My flesh trembles in fear of you;
I stand in awe of your laws.

DAY 2

The Covenant Family

The Lord asks us to love one another as He has loved us. When we are adopted into His family we suddenly have millions of brothers and sisters. How can we possibly love them all with the love of the Lord?

Obviously, we cannot "be there" for all of them in their time of need as God is, and we can't even know all of their names as He does. But we can, in so far as it lies within us, be at peace with our brothers and sisters—so that there is no division or discord in our body, particularly our local body. We can also have a generosity in spirit toward brothers and sisters of other denominations, cultures, and socioeconomic classes. We need to become world Christians by praying, supporting, and loving believers in other countries. Though other denominations may have different styles of worship or have different views on peripheral issues, as long as we agree on who Jesus is and why He came, we are covenant family, and we must love each other as brothers and sisters. Each denomination has beautiful strengths, and together, we truly do complete the body of Christ. I remember when Presbyterian Steve Brown addressed a crowd and said, "I am Reformed in my theology, and I love my denomination—but if I want prayer—I go to my charismatic brothers!" When we fail to see the strengths in one another, when we disparage one another, we not only hurt each other, we keep unbelievers from believing that what we have is real.

At the Last Supper, Jesus washed the feet of His disciples, vividly demonstrating how important humility is in loving well. When we feel we are superior to sisters in other churches, cultures, or even within our own local church, we cannot love well.

6. After washing their feet, Jesus gave His disciples a "new command." What was it, according to John 13:34?

7. How is this command different from the command to love our neighbor? What, according to John 13:35, will happen if this command is obeyed?

8. What did Jesus pray for in John 17:20-21 and why?

9. What do you think unbelievers feel when they observe fighting and a lack of grace within the body of Christ?

10. Do you think you love your covenant family well? Why or why not?

11. How about sisters in your own local church? How aware are you of their needs, their children, and their relationship to you as sisters?

DAY 3
Annuals and Perennials

Think about the differing types of flowers. There are annuals—the lovely but fragile petunias, pansies, and impatiens we put in our flower boxes, knowing they will brighten our lives for just a season. But then there are the hardy perennials—irises, tulips, or daisies that your grandmother may have planted and are still coming up faithfully each new spring. Most friends are like annual flowers, but annual flowers are valuable. They can be there during those times when perennials are not at their peak, adding color, variety, and beauty to our lives. For a season they bless you (or you them), but then they fade away and are gone, and even that is a blessing, for then there is room in your garden for new and different annuals!

But now and then God gives you a perennial—a friend who comes back season after season. You can't turn an annual into a perennial—a perennial is simply a gift from God. They are the "Ruths" and the "Jonathans" that God sends into your life to encourage you, love you, and stand by your side with unfailing love.

What is "unfailing love" in Scripture? The Hebrew word that is often translated unfailing love is *checed* or *hesed*. In this rich word two concepts are intertwined: mercy and steadfastness. God is not only merciful, He keeps on being merciful. Perhaps these two concepts are best expressed in Lamentations 3:22-23.

> *Because of the LORD's great love we are not consumed,*
> *for his compassions never fail.*
>
> *They are new every morning;*
> *great is your faithfulness.*

12. How did you see Ruth live out both mercy and steadfastness toward Naomi?

13. Not all friendships are perennial friendships. Can you think of some "annuals" in your life who are not in your life anymore, but who blessed you (or you them) for a time? What is the value of "annuals?"

Read 1 Samuel 18-20.

14. Summarize what happened in these three chapters.

15. Note the various ways Jonathan exemplifies unfailing love:

   A. 1 Samuel 18:3-4. What does Jonathan do? Remembering that Jonathan was next in line to be king, what was he communicating through his gifts to David?

   B. 1 Samuel 19:4-5. What does Jonathan do? At what risk to himself?

   C. What is David's concern and Jonathan's response in 1 Samuel 20:3-4?

   D. How do Jonathan's words in the above passage echo Ruth's words to Naomi in Ruth 3:5?

It is very difficult to ask for help, even when we are in great need, even when the friend is a "soul mate." I have found linguist Deborah Tannen's observations about the way women make requests fascinating. Tannen says we are much less direct than men because we are more concerned about "breaking connections." Rather than saying, "Could you take care of Tommy tomorrow while I go to the dentist?" many women will instead hint, saying, "I don't know what to do with Tommy while I'm at the dentist tomorrow." This teaches me to read between the lines when a friend shares a need with me, and if at all possible, to respond enthusiastically with an offer to help. Both Ruth and Jonathan responded with eagerness when their soul mates asked for help. "Whatever you ask me to do, I will do!" There is an implicit statement here that says, "I respect and love you so much—thank you for asking—I'm eager to meet your need!"

E. What promise does Jonathan make in 1 Samuel 20:12-13? At what risk to himself?

F. What promise does Jonathan ask from David in 1 Samuel 20:14-15?

Historically, it often happened that when a new king, outside of the family, came to power, the descendants of the old king were murdered so that there would be no threat to the throne. When David did come to power, the nurse for Jonathan's son thought they would come to kill the baby (Mephibosheth). (The story is in 2 Samuel 4:4 and 2 Samuel.)

16. What a tremendous risk Jonathan took for himself and his family when he supported David.

    A. How does Jonathan show unfailing love for David in 1 Samuel 20:41-42?

    B. How does he do it again in 1 Samuel 23:14-18?

17. What stands out to you from the life of Jonathan that you could apply in your soul mate or perennial friendships? Be specific.

DAY 4
. . . .

Should You Make a Friendship Covenant?

Both Jonathan and Ruth made a friendship promise to their soul mates. In the original edition of *The Friendships of Women* I suggested being open to making friendship promises with soul mates one had known a long time. However, I no longer advise it as a practice. Yes, it happened with Ruth and Naomi and also with David and Jonathan, but these friends faced exceptional stress, which is what I failed to take into account.

Would God ever lead us to make a vow? It is possible, in extremely rare circumstances. I promised my dear young friend Rita, who was twenty-three and dying, that I would be her friend and find a wife for her husband and a mother for her children. She pleaded with me, I promised, and God allowed me to fulfill my vow beautifully. But that kind of scenario is extremely rare. I have learned that it is better to be content with an implicit friendship vow than to make a verbal vow before God. Let me explain.

After my original edition of *The Friendships of Women* was released, I received some alarming mail and phone calls. One mother wrote me that her daughter read my book as a freshman at college and then made a lifelong friendship vow to her counselor, with whom she had been meeting for just one month! Another mother called me because she feared her daughter was getting into an unhealthy friendship with an older woman. This woman was discipling her and had asked her, on the basis of my book, to move in with her and make a promise of unfailing love to her. Whoa! Red flags waved at me. Both of the above examples shout to me, "relational idolatry!" Asking someone to bind herself to you with a vow after a short period of time is neither scriptural nor healthy. If someone is pressuring you to make a vow quickly, whether it is for friendship or for marriage—don't! Pressure comes from the father of lies, not the Holy Spirit. The enemy doesn't want us to slow down, think, pray, or wait on the Lord. Pressure to hurry and make a decision is one of his most common tricks. Don't fall for it.

Does God ever lead a person to make a verbal vow? Yes. In the case of marriage, God's Word is clear that He wants you to be true until death. In that case, the usual vows of love and faithfulness until death do not add to what God has already required of a couple, but is a reminder of that requirement. My friend Jan Silvious has explained to me that the word friendship comes from a root word meaning "free." One of the beautiful things about *friendship* is that it is free. God does not require us to maintain all friendships forever. It is not unusual for God to bring a very dear friend into your life for a season. When that season is passed, He may allow you to drift apart, though you may always feel a love for that person. But if you have vowed lifelong love to that friend, then you are bound to her, even though God might have loosed you! Sometimes it is hard for us to know, in our limited vision, if a friend is an annual or a perennial.

18. Find as many warnings as you can about vows in Ecclesiastes 5:1-6. What reasons are given for those warnings?

19. Describe the extraordinary circumstances that Ruth and Naomi faced and also David and Jonathan. Why might a vow have been important in these extraordinary circumstances?

However, though God's Word warns strongly against making hasty vows, there comes a time in a perennial friendship when being untrue will feel like betrayal, and, in fact, is. For both of you are aware of an "implicit" vow. Thirty-two years ago Lee and I bonded when the Lord used me as a vessel to bring Lee to Christ. Though we've been separated geographically for thirty years, we've nurtured our friendship through letters and e-mail. Lee has come to hear me speak many times. Many years ago, when I had not yet seen the danger of making friendship vows, she heard me suggest, when speaking in New York, the possibility of considering a friendship vow. That night Lee told me, earnestly, "I can't make a promise because I'm so afraid I would break it." I respected Lee's hesitancy, for it sprang out of a healthy fear of the Lord. I appreciate it all the more now. I am also confident of our implicit bond and our unspoken commitment to nurture it. As Lee and I rode in the airport bus to catch our separate planes, we felt the bittersweet pain of parting. Lee caught my hands in hers and said, "We are knit together, my friend. As Jonathan was knit to David, so I am knit to you."

Author Walter Wangerin says that vows don't have to be spoken in order for there to be a covenant between two people. He explains that every communal relationship is modeled on the primary relationship (God and man) and so has covenant in it. The covenant or code "is mostly unspoken, but both partners know it; and as long as both obey it, the relationship is protected and nourished as a living thing." When a close friend breaks that unspoken covenant by sharing your secrets, neglecting you in a time of great need, or committing another treachery, it hurts because it should. There has indeed been a trampling of life. Each of us needs to assess our implicit bonds. There are those who are going to feel rightfully let down if we fail them, even though no blood ties exist and no verbal promises have been made.

Action Assignment

Spend some time before God taking stock of those friends with whom there may be an "implicit vow." We obviously can't have many perennial friendships, but most of us have a few. Some good questions to ask are:

1. To whom have I been close for many years?

2. Is my soul knit to hers?

3. Is her soul knit to mine? (Friendship is free—you cannot insist on this.)

4. Would she feel rightfully let down if I were not there for her in a time of need?

5. Whom do You impress on my heart, Lord?

Make a list prayerfully and determine to be true. No vows need to be made. But implicit vows should be honored.

DAY 5

Amazing Grace

When a true soul mate friendship falls apart, it isn't usually due to neglect, for we tend to pay attention to the friends to whom we are knit. What causes soul mate friendships to wither is a failure to give grace. Some kind of betrayal or perceived betrayal will happen sooner or later because we all have feet of clay. This is when we, as sisters in Christ, have resources that secular friends do not have. This is when we can give the grace of unfailing love when others cannot.

You see, grace isn't natural, but supernatural. The natural responses when you get hurt are either to strike back or to withdraw. When we instead step out of the way and allow God to work through us, responding with unfailing love, even perennials that have endured a deep freeze may lift up their wilting heads and live.

In the midst of the original writing of this chapter, my soul mate, Shell, and I had a "freeze." I am knit to Shell, and she is the one friend to whom I have made a verbal vow (when I thought that was what Scripture modeled). Shortly after I vowed friendship to her, we had an awful argument! Mothers can become like mother bears when they are discussing "the right way" to raise children, and we both snarled, roared, and bared our teeth. I had always thought Shell was far too strict as a mother. I thought, *Why, Shell's girls aren't allowed to do anything!*

She thought, *Doesn't Dee know that boundaries are important in raising children?*

Today, twenty-five years later, we realize that God gave us each other, in part, to temper the other. We call ourselves "law" and "grace." That terrible day of our argument, neither one of us was slow to speak, quick to listen, or slow to become angry. Shell left my house in tears. I went to my husband, Steve, hoping for empathy, telling him of my hurt. Steve gently said, "I wonder if God is testing you."

"What do you mean?"

"Well, here you are in the midst of writing a book about the friendships of women. Now you have had a quarrel with a very dear friend. It seems this could be a test, an opportunity to live what you are teaching."

I was silent. I didn't like where this was going. But I also realized Steve really could be right. If he was, then I had better pass the test. I confess I sought God out at that point, not because of conviction, but because I was afraid that if I didn't He wouldn't bless the book I was writing. The sinner does not easily turn, but God in His mercy, can turn the sinner. And that's what He did—for when I was still before Him, He showed me my pride, cruelty, and insensitivity. I picked up the phone and called Shell. When she answered, I told her I was truly sorry. She was quiet, but then she thanked me for calling. I thought our friendship would quickly resume, but she stopped coming over, stopped calling. So, I went back to Steve. Surely now he would give me empathy! "I told Shell I was sorry. But she's freezing me out."

He put his arm around me. Encouraged, I said, "I don't think she realizes what a precious friend she might be losing in me." At that, Steve laughed!

Then he said, "I've heard you say that sometimes saying you are sorry isn't enough. Sometimes that can be remorse rather than repentance. You've said that sometimes you have to bear the fruit of repentance to convince the one you have wronged that you are truly sorry."

Again, I was silent. But, again, I tried. I wrote Shell a note telling her some of the reasons I loved her. When I still didn't hear from her, I baked her blueberry muffins as an excuse to go to her house. When she opened the door, we fell into each other's arms, weeping. She said, "Dee, I was going to forgive you—just not so quickly."

Then we laughed. How much we need God's help in our depravity! It is only through His power that we can give unfailing love.

Pray through Psalm 119:121-128 before you begin today's lesson. The psalmist was waiting for the Messiah, and for us, He has come. Yet often we wait for other manifestations of the Lord in our life, and we struggle against spiritual enemies. We may not feel we have done what is righteous and just, so then the psalm can be a springboard for confession. Pray responsively.

I have done what is righteous and just;
do not leave me to my oppressors.

Ensure your servant's well-being;
let not the arrogant oppress me.

My eyes fail, looking for your salvation,
looking for your righteous promise.

Deal with your servant according to your love
and teach me your decrees.

I am your servant; give me discernment
that I may understand your statutes.

It is time for you to act, O LORD;
your law is being broken.

Because I love your commands
more than gold, more than pure gold,

and because I consider all your precepts right,
I hate every wrong path.

20. If you read chapter 9 of *The Friendships of Women*, what stood out to you?

21. When you have been hurt by a friend, what tends to be your natural response?

In *What's So Amazing about Grace*, Philip Yancey says that grace is amazing because it's not natural.

22. Read Matthew 18:21-35.

    A. What is Peter's question to Jesus?

B. How does Jesus answer? What does this mean?

C. Summarize the story Jesus tells.

D. What is the central point of the story?

E. What severe warning comes in verse 35?

F. The *New American Standard* translates verse 35: "My heavenly Father will also do the same to you, if each of you does not forgive his brother from your heart." What do you think it means to forgive "from your heart"?

G. What keeps us from forgiving one another?

How is God leading you to apply this week's lesson? How do you need His help?

PRAYER TIME

Cluster in groups of three or four. Have each woman lift up a confession or need of her heart, perhaps stimulated by the last question, and then allow the others to support her. When there is a pause, another woman should lift up her need.

Next week's lesson is long. Get started early. Your group may choose to divide it.

Ten

Roses and Alligators

We long for unfailing love, and we can ask the Lord to help us show it and receive it. But we must also realize that we are all sinners, and despite the best of intentions, we are going to let each other down. Genuine friends are like roses—breathtakingly lovely and worth the pain of an occasional surprising jab from a hidden thorn.

There are people, however, who look like roses, but aren't roses at all. They are alligators. Can you tell the difference between a rose and an alligator?

DAY I

Alligators Demonstrate a Pattern of Betrayal

The difference between a rose and an alligator is that a rose may never hurt you, but an alligator is likely to destroy you. Alligators demonstrate a pattern of destruction. Every rose has a few thorns, but an alligator is covered with them. His smile reveals jagged teeth lining his long snout. From the back of his neck to the muscled whip of his tail run rough, dangerous barbs. Your chances of escaping major injury if you cozy up to an alligator are slim. What should you do if God has allowed an alligator in your life—especially if he or she is up close and personal—such as an employer, a parent, or a spouse? The alligator in David's life was the father of his best friend, his employer, and the King of Israel, King Saul. Saul gives us a portrait of an alligator, and David models what to do if one is in your life.

An alligator's thorns, unlike the thorns of a rose, are life-threatening, putting your spiritual, emotional, or physical life in jeopardy. Experts testify that three acts of violence in an abusive situation is evidence of a pattern.

Prepare your heart by praying responsively through Psalm 119:129-136.

Your statutes are wonderful;
   therefore I obey them.

The unfolding of your words gives light;
   it gives understanding to the simple.

I open my mouth and pant,
   longing for your commands.

Turn to me and have mercy on me,
   as you always do to those who love your name.

Direct my footsteps according to your word;
   let no sin rule over me.

Redeem me from the oppression of men,
   that I may obey your precepts.

Make your face shine upon your servant
   and teach me your decrees.

Streams of tears flow from my eyes,
   for your law is not obeyed.

WARMUP

Women can be like roses, breathtakingly lovely in so many ways! Yet underneath our glossy green leaves are some surprisingly nasty thorns. What are some thorns in your life that you long for the Lord to prune, which tend to stick your loved ones? (Hear from just a few who are willing to make themselves vulnerable!)

1. Read through 1 Samuel 18—20, and note each time Saul tries to kill David.

2. What did Jesus say in Matthew 7:19-21?

3. Read 1 Samuel 19:6-11. Describe Saul's words. Describe his actions. Does the "fruit" of his actions support his words?

4. Read 1 Samuel 24.

   A. What was Saul doing in verses 1-2?

B. What does David do to Saul, and how does David feel in verses 3-7?

C. What are David's words in verses 8-11? What are his actions? Does the "fruit" of his actions support his words?

D. What is David's prayer to God in verses 12-13?

E. In verses 14-21, what are Saul's words?

F. According to 1 Samuel 26:1-2, does Saul keep his word?

DAY 2

A Fool Is Right in His Own Eyes

A more accurate scriptural term than alligator is the word *fool*. I'll never forget the first time I heard good teaching on the concept of a "fool" in Scripture. I was sharing the platform with *Fool-Proofing Your Life* author, Jan Silvious. (She has since told me, "I think I was born to write that book.") It has helped so many people who work for a fool, gave birth to a fool, or are married to a fool.

Before Jan's book, I was always quick to advise young women struggling in their marriages to stay and submit. Now I realize I have at times sent a fawn right into the jaws of an alligator. I now draw her out with questions. If her husband exhibits the following characteristics of a fool—abusive, addicted, or faithless—the kind thing and the only real hope for their marriage, is instead to say: "Separate. Set boundaries. Insist he get help and show change before you go back. You and your children are not safe. Flee."

It is important, however, for our own sake, as well as the fool's, to forgive him or her, as David did Saul—from our hearts. But there is no sin in putting space between yourself and a fool as Jan Silvious illustrates with a castle and a moat. Imagine you are in your castle when a fool comes near. Be polite, wave, smile, but pull up your drawbridge. Don't welcome a fool into your life, for he reaps destruction.

One day I was driving through the drive-through of a fast food restaurant. There was a sign at the speaker that said, "The speaker is broken. Drive up to the window and place your order."

I drove up to the window where there was a large, scowling red-headed man. He yelled at me: **"WHY DIDN'T YOU ORDER IN THE SPEAKER?"**

Though taken aback, I replied, "Because there was a sign saying your speaker was broken."

His eyes flared: **"THE SPEAKER'S NOT BROKEN!"**

"Then perhaps you should take your sign down," I suggested, hoping a soft word would turn away wrath.

His face grew red, and veins in his neck throbbed as he yelled: **"I'M NOT GOING TO TAKE THE SIGN DOWN JUST BECAUSE YOU TELL ME TO TAKE IT DOWN!"**

Because I had learned, from the book of Proverbs, the tell-tale signs of a fool, I thought, *Pull your drawbridge up, Dee*. I didn't try to reason anymore with him, for I know a fool is always right in his own eyes, uses anger to control, and can become violent. I put distance between me and him, for a wise person sees danger and goes the other way. I pushed the button on my automatic window, closed the space between me and the fool, and drove away. I did forgive him, and I truly have learned to feel compassion for fools, for I know their end is destruction. But, like David, I fled.

Jesus warns sternly against calling your *brother* a fool (Matt. 5:22). In fact, it is not likely that a true Christian could be a fool, for the fear of God helps us to see ourselves as we are, sinners in need of repentance and grace. True Christians will behave foolishly at times, but they do not demonstrate the *pattern* of destruction, the complete obsession with self that a fool does.

Begin today by praying responsively through Psalm 119:137-144. May our heart by like the psalmist's and not the fool's.

Righteous are you, O Lord,
  and your laws are right.

The statutes you have laid down are righteous;
  they are fully trustworthy.

My zeal wears me out,
  for my enemies ignore your words.

Your promises have been thoroughly tested,
  and your servant loves them.

Though I am lowly and despised,
  I do not forget your precepts.

Your righteousness is everlasting
  and your law is true.

Trouble and distress have come upon me,
  but your commands are my delight.

Your statutes are forever right;
  give me understanding that I may live.

5. A fool may act religious to gain favor with man and even use words of repentance, but he doesn't mean them. What does a fool truly believe, in his heart, according to Psalm 14:1?

6. Give an example of Saul using words of repentance. Then give evidence that he didn't mean those words.

7. Sometimes a person isn't a fool, but will, in a few instances, act foolishly. (Haven't we all?) It is also possible that rather than dealing with a fool, we are dealing with someone who is immature. What does Proverbs 22:15 teach? Why does this person have more hope than a fool?

8. If we see the signs we are about to study repeatedly in someone, then, for our own safety, we should keep a polite distance. What does Proverbs 13:20 teach?

It is important not to label people hastily as fools, for we all have a sin nature, and we all behave foolishly at times. But if you see a pattern of the following characteristics then, for your own safety, you must set boundaries.

9. Discover the characteristic of a fool from the following passages. Sometimes there is a contrast with a wise person, which will help in your understanding. Write down the warning about the fool in a word or two that will be easy for you to remember.

A. *Some became fools through their rebellious ways and suffered affliction because of their iniquities.* Psalm 107:17

Characteristic?

B. *The way of a fool is right in his own eyes, but a wise man is he who listens to counsel.* Proverbs 12:15 (NAS).

Characteristic?

C. *The fear of the LORD is the beginning of knowledge, but fools despise wisdom and discipline.* Proverbs 1:7

Characteristic?

D. *The wise in heart accept commands, but a chattering fool comes to ruin.* Proverbs 10:8

Characteristic?

E. *He who conceals his hatred has lying lips, and whoever spreads slander is a fool.* Proverbs 10:8

Characteristic?

F. *A fool shows his annoyance at once, but a prudent man overlooks an insult.* Proverbs 12:16

Characteristic?

G. *A longing fulfilled is sweet to the soul, but fools detest turning from evil.* Proverbs 13:19

Characteristic?

H. *The wisdom of the prudent is to understand his way, But the folly of fools is deceit.* Proverbs 14:8 (NKJV).

Characteristic?

I. *A wise man fears the LORD and shuns evil, but a fool is hotheaded and reckless.* Proverbs 14:16

Characteristic?

J. *The tongue of the wise commends knowledge, but the mouth of the fool gushes folly.* Proverbs 15:2

Characteristic?

K. *A rebuke impresses a man of discernment more than a hundred lashes a fool.* Proverbs 17:10

Characteristic?

L. *A fool finds no pleasure in understanding but delights in airing his own opinions.* Proverbs 18:2

Characteristic?

M. *A fool's lips bring him strife, and his mouth invites a beating.* Proverbs 18:6

Characteristic?

N. *It is to a man's honor to avoid strife, but every fool is quick to quarrel.* Proverbs 20:3

Characteristic?

O. *As a dog returns to its vomit, so a fool repeats his folly.* Proverbs 26:11

Characteristic?

As much as we would hope that someone who has hurt us deeply would repent, if he or she is a fool, it won't happen. Instead, he will go on hurting people, repeating his folly. A wise person will keep her distance.

10. Summarize, in a few phrases, the signs of a fool.

11. How did David deal with the fool in his life? How should you?

DAY 3

Boundaries

Another series of books that has had a tremendous impact on many lives, including mine, is the *Boundaries* series by Dr. Henry Cloud and Dr. John Townsend. Again, with Scripture as their base, they show how relationships can remain (or become) healthy by setting boundaries. Boundaries can offer protection against fools, though they probably will not change a fool (for a fool thinks he is never wrong). However, roses will often respond to boundaries and with the weeds removed, become healthier and more beautiful.

I treated a rose like an alligator once. I fled when I should have set a boundary. April was sending her toddlers over to our house every day, all day. After six months of this, I began to plead with Steve to move to another part of the city. He finally agreed. It was a very expensive and unnecessary solution because April wasn't an alligator. April was not trying to destroy anyone. It was just that toddlers drove her crazy, and she knew I loved kids. I'd told her so! What I never had the courage to tell her was that I also needed to have some time with my children by themselves, and so I would love having her children sometimes. I think she would have been agreeable to working out a schedule. Instead of being clear, I dropped hints. My failure to confront led to flight, a dropped friendship, and large moving bills. I handled it poorly. (And my sister Sally wisely said, "Don't you realize what you've done? Your failure to confront encouraged April in her sin.")

"Boundaries," Cloud and Townsend explain, "define us. They define what is me and what is not me." In the above example, a boundary with April would have been to request that we each take care of our own children. We could exchange play-dates, but we each should primarily be responsible for our own children. When the children came knocking at a time not prearranged, I would have needed to enforce the boundary by saying, "I'm sorry, we don't have a play-date today. You need to go home now." If they didn't go home, I would have needed to walk them home and gently explain what happened to April. Difficult? Yes. But boundaries are actually much kinder than flight. That mature choice might very well have pruned the weed that was choking my friendship with April.

Today we'll consider a few basic principles in helping us understand and use boundaries.

12. Carrying an Overburden versus Carrying an Everyday Load

A. What does Galatians 6:2 command?

A *burden*, in the Greek means an "oppressive burden," an unusually heavy load, too much for one person. When Naomi lost her land, husband, and sons, she was devastated. Because of her dramatic losses, the basic needs of life became too much for her, and Ruth came alongside and helped her.

B. What are some ways Ruth helped Naomi carry her burden?

C. Give some examples of circumstances that would indicate a friend might be over-burdened.

D. What does Galatians 6:5 command?

A "load" in the Greek means an everyday load. We shouldn't expect help with these loads, and we aren't really helping people when we step in and carry their everyday loads, for we are teaching them irresponsibility. (This was one of my mistakes with my neighbor April, for God wanted her, rather than me, to raise her children.)

E. Give some examples of everyday loads.

F. Imagine that a friend or a child was in the habit of asking you to do something that she could do easily for herself? What would be the loving response?

13. Sowing and Reaping

A. What does Galatians 6:7 say?

B. What do you think it means to try to mock God? Why is this impossible in the long run?

C. According to Galatians 6:8, what will the person who sows to the flesh reap? The person who sows to the Spirit?

D. Looking back at Galatians 5:19-21, give some examples of the works of the flesh.

E. In the following examples, explain first, how a misguided believer might try to interrupt the natural consequence of a friend's poor choices. Then, explain how a true friend would draw a boundary so that the God-given law of sowing and reaping could occur.

You have a friend with a drinking problem who is missing work. She asks you to cover for her to your mutual employer.

Your friend abuses credit cards and comes to you for financial help.

Boundaries force the person who is doing the sowing to also do the reaping...Confronting an irresponsible person is not painful to him; only consequences are.
Dr. Henry Cloud and Dr. John Townsend, *Boundaries*, (Zondervan), p. 85.

F. What exhortations are in Galatians 6:9-10? How does this support the principle of sowing and reaping?

14. The Law of Motivation

Cloud and Townsend say that Christians often have trouble setting boundaries because it may seem unloving. Yet often what truly motivates us to live without boundaries is not love but fear. A friend fears confronting her friend, so she continues putting up with long phone calls at dinner or during her evening time with her husband. A parent fears his adult child's anger, so he pays his bills while his adult child doesn't work.

A. Share a time when the consequences of your behavior helped you to change your behavior.

B. Why is it important to look at our motivations for "helping" someone?

15. Boundaries Reveal Character

The way an individual responds to a reasonable boundary will often reveal her character. If she is a fool, she will insist on breaking the boundary. But if she is a rose, she may feel hurt, but she will consider the boundary, receive it (either immediately or in time), and discover that it has a positive effect, not only on her, but also on the friendship. Boundaries release folly from fools and fragrance from roses.

A. Consider how King Saul responded to the boundaries set. What do you see in 1 Samuel 19:4-10? What does this tell you about him?

B. Consider how Jonathan responded to the boundary set in 1 Samuel 20:1-4. What does this tell you about him?

C. Ruth set a boundary for Naomi when Naomi tried to send her back to Moab. Ruth knew this wasn't in either her or Naomi's best interest, and she insists on going with her. In time, how did Naomi respond? What does this tell you about Naomi?

DAY 4

Roses

When a friend lets us down, we show that our theology is off base when we're overcome with shock. The Bible teaches that we're all going to let each other down. Even the most beautiful rose has thorns. Professor Greg Scharf of Trinity Seminary says, "When someone fails you, don't be stunned! It's more appropriate to think, Hmmmm! That confirms what Scripture teaches—that we're all sinners, that there's none that is righteous, no, not one."

Charles Schultz, the creator of the Peanuts cartoons, knew the Lord. Every fall he repeated the strip in which Luci convinces Charlie Brown to trust her and let her hold the football for him. Every fall Charlie Brown falls flat on his back. The point? We are human. Sooner or later, we will fail each other even if we truly love that person. We need to mature to the point where our dependence is in God alone—for only He is without sin, and only He will never let us down, never move away, and never die.

This doesn't mean, however, that we should not love and cherish roses. A dedicated rose gardener, when stuck by the thorn of a rose, doesn't give up on roses. He learns how to deal with the thorns, and so must we. There are some scriptural principles to help us.

16. Don't Take Offenses Personally

A rose doesn't necessarily bear personal animosity. She simply was born with thorns. Often the hurt we receive from other people is not due to their feelings about us, but due to the selfish and sinful nature we all have. We all struggle with bad habits and sins, and while we may fully realize that our messiness, tardiness, or even addiction is a hurtful habit, we are not directing that hurt toward a person, but instead, struggling to overcome an engrained pattern of behavior. Our thorns may also be a result of a storm in our lives. Hurt people hurt people. Consider Naomi.

A. Why do you think Naomi kept sending her daughters-in-law back to Moab? Was it because she didn't like them? Explain, supporting your answer scripturally.

B. Why did Naomi say she'd come back empty when Ruth was right at her side?

C. Why do you think Ruth was able to persist instead of retreating when she was jabbed by this thorn?

17. **Walk in Humility**

Recently a dear friend accused me of thinking that I was better than the other women in our church. Her words hurt. Yet I knew I needed to take this before the Lord to see if it was true. It turned out that in this particular case she was mistaken, and we discovered her thinking was based on a misunderstanding of something she thought I had done that I hadn't. Yet, I also realized that she could have been right, for pride is a big problem in my life. Our associate pastor, Allen Taha, said, "When someone accuses you of something you should reply, "You don't know the half of it!" We all have such a strong sin nature—how much better to realize they may very well be right, for our depravity is strong. We must take every criticism before God and sift out the chaff from the wheat to learn from our critics.

A. In Proverbs 12:15-16, what are the differences between a fool and a wise man?

B. When you are criticized, how do you typically respond?

C. What does Proverbs 27:6 teach? Share a wound from a friend that you trusted and grew from.

D. List the commands given to us in Ephesians 4:1-3. How are they related to each other?

18. **Reflect on the Beauty of the Rose after You Have Been Stuck by Her Thorn**

When my friend accused me, it was tempting to simply flee the relationship. But I thought about how she had loved me well in the past. She had prepared a beautiful meal for our family, had been there for me when Steve was sick, and wept with me when he died. She had loved my children, taking them out for lunch, mentoring them, and listening to their hearts. She had prayed for my concerns. She and her husband are raising beautiful children who love the Lord deeply. Was I really going to throw away this friendship on the basis of one incident? As I reflected on her loveliness, I knew I was willing to put up with her thorns.

A. What does 1 Peter 4:8 teach?

B. When you fail people you love, how do you hope they think about you?

19. **Realize Our Enemy May Be on the Prowl**

Satan is like a wolf who schemes to divide the sheep, for he knows that united we stand, divided we fall. He likes to have us withdraw from one another so that he can pluck us off, one by one. He is not kind but attacks when we are down. When my friend accused me, I was down—grieving the loss of Steve. Our church had also been suffering, losing members over misunderstandings. I realized, in praying over the situation, that this very well could be the enemy, for he is the author of confusion. I was determined not to let him win. He would not succeed in causing more division in our church.

A. In 2 Corinthians 2:8-11, what does Paul urge and why?

B. How can a lack of forgiveness play into the enemy's hands?

C. How does Jesus describe our enemy in John 8:44?

D. How does Peter describe him in 1 Peter 5:8?

E. How can realizing that our enemy is real help you be more forgiving toward your sisters in Christ?

20. **Remember How Much You Have Been Forgiven**

Perhaps this is the most important principle of all.

A. What does Ephesians 4:32 teach?

B. List some of the things for which Jesus has completely forgiven you.

DAY 5
. . . .

How to Apologize

We will let our dearest friends down. Born with thorns, we must learn how to apologize well, for it is something we should do often in our lives. Yet very few people apologize well. As Solomon says, "a faithful friend is very rare." Faithfulness doesn't mean we won't fail, since we all have a sin nature and will let one another down. Faithfulness does mean that we will be sincerely repentant and do the U-Turn when our sin hurts another. What do faithful friends do when they hurt another?

They call or come in person, confessing their sin, with no excuses. (Excuses cancel the apology, for the blame has been shifted. If there were unusual circumstances, God can prompt the hurt person to inquire, but a true apology isn't: "I'm sorry, but…".)

They acknowledge exactly how their action has caused pain.

They make amends. True repentance bears fruit. It does the U-Turn.

My friend Shell and I have hurt each other and needed to humble ourselves in true repentance. Once, she broke my confidence, but she was at my house that very day, tearful, telling me exactly what she had done, with no excuses. She was heartbroken that she'd hurt me and promised to never to it again—and she hasn't.

My husband Steve was a faithful friend. Once in Sunday school he teased me, making comments about my driving. I told him, after church, that I had been embarrassed. I'll never forget the look of pain in his eyes. He told me a little later how convicted he had been, how much he loved me, and how sorry he was to have hurt me. He then made it a point to brag about me in Sunday school! Oh, such a dear man.

It takes humility to confess with no excuses and to make amends. Humility does not come naturally; it takes an act of grace. In our depravity, we quickly offer excuses for ourselves, we minimize the pain we've caused, and we don't want to bear fruit worthy of repentance. I struggle with this every time I hurt someone.

When we were living in Seattle, I was trying to teach our new puppy, "Darling," to stay in our yard without a fence. But honestly, I had gotten sloppy, wasn't watching her, and instead, was absorbed in a book I was reading. Suddenly, I heard the angry cries of my neighbor. "GET OUT! SCAT! YOU $#+&# DOG!!!!!!" I looked up, alarmed, to see Darling digging in her beautiful rhododendrons. I knew my neighbor loved her flowers.

Help me, God. I ran over, scooped up our puppy, and said, "I'm so sorry!" He helped me make no excuses.

But before I could acknowledge the pain my negligence had caused, my neighbor stormed into her house, slamming the door behind her. I retreated up our path with Darling. I knew I needed to bear fruit worthy of repentance. My husband often had received fish from his patients. So I went to our freezer, took out a salmon, and headed back to my neighbor's. When she opened the door, I said, "I'm so sorry I didn't watch my puppy. I know you have worked so hard on your flowers. I wanted to give you this salmon."

She surprised me by saying: "Fish! I've got a freezer full of fish! That's the last thing I need." Then she closed the door in my face.

Embarrassed, I retreated again. In the safety of my house, I curled up in an overstuffed chair and nursed my wounds, telling the Lord that I had tried. After all, Darling was just a puppy—wasn't my neighbor partly to blame for being so intolerant? And I had apologized—wasn't my neighbor now the one who was in the wrong? "Lord," I asked, "Isn't the ball in her court now?"

Instead of comforting me, He brought Romans 12:18 to mind: "If it is possible, as far as it depends on you, live at peace with everyone."

Do I really have to try again? I sat there, stubbornly. I am convinced that our Lord has a great sense of humor, for at that moment, the UPS truck pulled up in front. The man carried a crate of beautiful Florida oranges and grapefruit to our door—a gift from my mother-in-law. Moments later I was headed back to my neighbor's with a cardboard tray of citrus fruit.

After ringing the doorbell, I stood there, nervously. This time, when she opened the door, she was the astonished one. After a long silence, she broke into a grin. "You don't give up, do you, honey?" She took the fruit and walked away, shaking her head and chuckling.

I learned so much from this experience, for my relationship with that neighbor was warm and good from that moment on. She hadn't been particularly friendly before, but now she smiled and waved when I drove into the driveway.

21. Describe an effective and ineffective apology.

22. Read Luke 15:11-24

    A. How did the younger son cause pain to his father?

    B. What did he say when he apologized? Did he offer excuses?

    C. How did he show he was willing to bear fruit worthy of repentance?

    D. How did the father receive him?

23. In Isaiah 66:2, whom does the Lord esteem? How are these qualities related to apologizing well?

24. What was needed for repentance to be true in the following incidents?
    A. Isaiah 58:3

    B. Luke 3:7-8

25. What is the promise of James 4:10?

26. Is there someone to whom you should give a true apology? If so, pray about a plan and then do it.

27. If you read chapter 10 of *The Friendships of Women*, what do you remember from it?

PRAYER TIME

Cluster in groups of three or four. Have each woman lift up a confession or need of her heart, and then allow the others to support her. When there is a pause, another woman should lift up her need.

Eleven

God Knows Our Needs Better than We Do

So often we read the story of Mary and Elizabeth's friendship at Christmas time. How important it is at other times, especially when studying the friendships of women, to study this amazing friendship and to see how God knew the needs of Elizabeth and Mary, better than they did—and how He orchestrated their three-month visit.

DAY 1

The Miracle of Friendship

In an article in *Partnership*, Isabel Anders writes of her solitary trip to London:

> *I had been seeing a play a day, alone. I didn't realize how lonely I was, mingling with crowds and speaking only to waitresses, cab drivers, clerks, and ticket agents. I certainly wasn't looking for a friend on my last afternoon before returning home.*

Before the play, Isabel had lunch in the theatre tea shop. The shop was crowded, so the host asked Isabel if she would mind sharing her table with Sibyl, whom Isabel described as a sweet-faced Englishwoman. They chatted and sipped tea companionably, each enjoying the other's company. Then they parted, each to find her theatre seat. When Isabel found her seat, she was startled to see that Sibyl had the seat next to her! Sibyl seemed very glad, saying it was "fated." Isabel wrote, reflectively: "I tend to be solitary and had not realized my own need to interact with someone deeply. I began to catch on that God was giving me the gift of a friend."

The play was an intensely moving one, the subject being commitment in marriage and the perils of a lack of commitment. It was a meaningful theme to each woman: Isabel was then dating the man who would be her future husband, and Sibyl was married to a "man who had been (and had put her) through much grief." Touched by the play, each woman glanced at the other occasionally. Sibyl was close to tears. After the play, Isabel and Sibyl waited in the lobby for a violent storm to subdue. The play and their sensitivity to God's hand helped them to share their lives vulnerably with each other. They discovered many threads binding them together, including the fact that they were sisters in Christ. Isabel was encouraged by the beauty of Sibyl's faith over adversity, writing:

> *The triumph of grace over adversity and God's care for her as an individual shone through, as sweetly as I've ever seen in a human face. I felt renewed strength for the life that was ahead of me—whatever it might be. How calmly we walk into the miracles of our lives—and to me, friendship is one of those miracles! How, out of all the people of the streets of London, should Sibyl and I encounter each other? God knew my needs and Sibyl's better than we had known ourselves.*

WARMUP

Share a time when you suspected God was giving you the gift of a friend. What makes you think God was involved?

1. As an overview, read Luke 1:1-58. Look for similarities in circumstances between Elizabeth and Mary. Write down everything you discover.

2. Look again at the following verses, comparing one to another. What commonalities do you see that might have given these women empathy for each other?

   A. Luke 1:7 and Matthew 1:19

   B. Luke 1:18-20 and Matthew 1:19-21

   C. Luke 1:13 and Luke 1:31

   D. Luke 1:25 and Luke 1:48

   E. Luke 1:57-58 and Luke 2:6-7; Luke 2:16-19

DAY I
. . . .

Waiting on God for Friendship

How often we see God making His children wait. Sometimes they had to wait as long as forty years to see a promise fulfilled. Some had to wait until heaven. In these opening chapters of Luke, we see how long Elizabeth and Zechariah waited for a baby, and how long Simeon and Anna waited to see the Messiah. Waiting on God is something believers must do.

In the same way, God often makes us wait for friendship. This is a pattern we see in the scriptural models we are studying. They all had to wait for friends. Ruth had to wait for Naomi to appreciate her, David and Jonathan endured childhoods of loneliness, and Elizabeth waited five months for someone who would really understand and would also be able to talk to her! (Her husband, Zechariah, had been struck dumb for the duration of her pregnancy.)

Every time Steve and I moved, I asked God to give me a soul mate right away! He never did it *right away*. He always made me wait. Perhaps in His love He makes us wait so we will depend on Him. Loneliness can make you do that. Then, at just the right time, He sends a friend. He knows our needs better than we do. When I look back over my life, and I am a grandmother now, I realize my most precious women friends were friends I asked God for, but also had to wait for. When I ran ahead of Him, initiating friendships without seeking Him, the friendships were "clay" instead of "gold."

How obvious it is that Elizabeth's dependency was on God. I think if I had been Elizabeth my first response after having waited so long for a baby would have been to run out and tell my women friends. Her first response was to go into seclusion with God. Most commentators believe that time was spent in preparation, much as Manoah's wife in Judges had to prepare herself to be the Samson's mother. Elizabeth was a worshiper, and God blessed her, not only with Himself, but also with an incredible friend who would understand carrying a miracle baby. Both mothers would face incredible pain in the future, and God used them to strengthen each other for the journey.

In the octrain from Psalm 119 today there is a passage about waiting, morning and night. This is one that my husband and I loved and is set to music in the CD in *A Woman of Worship*. In the *New King James* version it is:

I rise before the dawning of the morning,
    And cry for help;
    I hope in Your word.
My eyes are awake through the night watches,
    That I may meditate on Your word.

Psalm 119:147-148

This isn't just passive waiting—this is crying for help and meditating on His Word. That's what I imagine Elizabeth doing those five months. No wonder she uttered her amazing prophecy when Mary came for her famous visit.

Pray through this octrain from Psalm 119:145-152, lifting to Him whatever you are waiting for:

I call with all my heart; answer me, O Lord,
    and I will obey your decrees.

I call out to you; save me
    and I will keep your statutes.

I rise before dawn and cry for help;
I have put my hope in your word.

My eyes stay open through the watches of the night,
that I may meditate on your promises.

Hear my voice in accordance with your love;
preserve my life, O Lord, according to your laws.

Those who devise wicked schemes are near,
but they are far from your law.

Yet you are near, O Lord,
and all your commands are true.

Long ago I learned from your statutes
that you established them to last forever.

In each of our scriptural models, waiting for friends and love can be seen. Often it is "active" waiting, that is, waiting that is combined with trust, prayer, fasting, pondering Scripture, and being alone with God, seeking Him.

3. Consider Ruth and Naomi.

   A. Approximately how long did Ruth have to wait before Naomi responded more enthusiastically to her commitment of friendship? (Clues can be found in Ruth 1:22 and Ruth 2:23.)

   B. If Ruth left for the threshing room floor at dusk, how long did she have to wait until Boaz awakened? (Ruth 3:8) Imagine her thoughts and prayers to God!

   C. What commands to wait does Ruth receive from both Boaz and Naomi in Ruth 3:10-16?

Can you imagine Ruth's thoughts when she had to wait many hours for Boaz to awaken, and then had to wait a day to see if this man of her dreams would be free to marry her or if she would end up with the other closer kinsman? I see amazing trust in Ruth, rekindled faith in Naomi when she tells Ruth to wait, and God coming through for these waiting women. He gave Ruth, not a Moabite man, not a selfish man, but a godly man who truly cared for her. One application I see from this story is that if God is in a relationship, He will make it happen, and though we should cooperate with God, we shouldn't try to force His hand, or we may end up with the wrong man or the wrong friend.

In the musical *Brigadoon*, Fiona's friends chastise her for waiting so long for the right man, telling her that without a man, how long is the night! Aptly she sings back, that the night is much longer if the man's not right!

D. What do you learn about waiting from Ruth's model?

E. Internet dating has entered our culture. If you think this is an appropriate channel for marriage, how might the principle of waiting be important?

4. Consider David and Jonathan.

A. In his psalms, David often is waiting, but it is active waiting. Describe how he waits according to Psalm 5:1-3? How could you follow this model?

B. What enables David to wait, according to Psalm 25:1-5? How do you see active waiting?

Sara Groves wrote a song called "Cave of Adullum." In it David is crying out to God, as we see him doing in the Psalms, asking God to speak to him, because his life has not turned out as he expected! He had been anointed to be the next king of Israel, and yet, he is living on the run, hiding in caves, deserts, and forests so that Saul doesn't murder him. What David constantly does in his waiting is to ask God to remind him of the vision, to give him a sense of God's presence, and to help him to trust while he waits. I so identify! How many times things have gone differently than I expected, and disappointment is deep. I wait on God and remind myself of His promises. So often, just when you think you can't wait anymore, He strengthens you.

C. To where did David escape in 1 Samuel 22:1? And where was he hiding (1 Sam. 23:14-15)?

D. In 1 Samuel 23:16-18, how did God strengthen David? Find as much as you can.

5. Consider Mary and Elizabeth.

   A. How long had Elizabeth and Zechariah prayed for a baby? (For clues see Luke 1:7 and 1:36.)

There is a pattern when Scripture says a woman "had not" a child and then God "gave her" a child. The resulting awaited child is always a child of significance. Consider Isaac, Joseph, Samson, and Samuel.

   B. What did Gabriel say to Zechariah in Luke 1:13?

This makes me smile. It could have been thirty years since they had stopped praying for a baby! Yet Gabriel appears and says, "Your prayer has been heard," as if they had prayed yesterday! Did Zechariah think, *What prayer?*

   C. How did God discipline Zechariah for his words, which showed a lack of faith? (Luke 1:18-20)

   D. How might have Zechariah's discipline been hard for Elizabeth at this time as well? How did she respond to all that had happened? Why? (Luke 1:24)

   E. How does God bless Elizabeth after her time of seclusion?

6. What do you learn about waiting on God from these models? About waiting on God in friendship?

7. How will you apply what you have learned?

One of my favorite Christmas carols is "O Come, O Come Emmanuel." I love its haunting melody and yearning lyrics. This "waiting" is what characterized the saints we see in Luke 1 and 2: Elizabeth, Zechariah, Mary, Anna, and Simeon. There was so much injustice, so much suffering—and yet, there was the promise of a Messiah.

Read through Psalm 119:153-160. There is sadness and anger, but also a steady beat of hope in God and His promises. This situation may not be yours now, but you can pray for someone who is hurting. You may be shocked by the verse that says, "I look on the faithless with loathing," for we are commanded to love our neighbor, no matter the state of her heart. Many of the Psalms are prayers against Israel's enemies, and we can apply these psalms by looking at our spiritual enemies, the forces of darkness.

Look upon my suffering and deliver me,
*   for I have not forgotten your law.*

Defend my cause and redeem me;
*   preserve my life according to your promise.*

Salvation is far from the wicked,
*   for they do not seek out your decrees.*

Your compassion is great, O Lord;
*   preserve my life according to your laws.*

Many are the foes who persecute me,
*   but I have not turned from your statutes.*

I look on the faithless with loathing,
*   for they do not obey your word.*

See how I love your precepts;
*   preserve my life, O Lord, according to your love.*

All your words are true;
*   all your righteous laws are eternal.*

DAY 3

I Am the Lord's Servant

There seems to be two common and erroneous extremes in considering Mary. The first is to consider her a demi-goddess and elevate her too much. As John Macarthur says in his book, *Twelve Extraordinary Women*:

> *She is never portrayed in Scripture as a source or dispenser of grace, but is herself the recipient of God's grace.*

In talking to a friend who does pray to Mary, she told me that it isn't that she sees Mary as divine, but that she is giving another believer, Mary, her prayer request. I understand, for I have asked Jesus to ask my late husband to pray for our children—yet, I don't think others are asking Steve to intercede for them. As I said to my friend, "Mary probably gets millions of prayer requests every day. What person can effectively handle that?"

Macarthur says that "Those who channel their religious energies into the veneration of Mary would do well to learn from the example of Mary herself. God is the only one she magnified."

On the other hand, we can fall into the other extreme. Luci Shaw believes we have abandoned Mary to an "evangelical limbo." Convinced that many Catholics erroneously worship Mary, many Protestants fall into the opposite error: They ignore her, except at Christmas when she is dusted off and placed in their nativity scenes. But Mary has so much to teach us. Truly, she was a worshiper of God, which also made her an amazing friend. Artists and poets have tried to capture the Annunciation from Luke 1. Because this is such a familiar passage, read it this time, in *The Message*.

[26]*In the sixth month of Elizabeth's pregnancy, God sent the angel Gabriel to the Galilean village of Nazareth* [27]*to a virgin engaged to be married to a man descended from David. His name was Joseph, and the virgin's name, Mary.* [28]*Upon entering, Gabriel greeted her:*

> *Good morning!*
>
> *You're beautiful with God's beauty,*
>
> *Beautiful inside and out!*
>
> *God be with you.*

[29]*She was thoroughly shaken, wondering what was behind a greeting like that.* [30]*But the angel assured her, "Mary, you have nothing to fear. God has a surprise for you:* [31]*You will become pregnant and give birth to a son and call his name Jesus.*

> [32]*He will be great,*
>
>   *be called "Son of the Highest.'*
>
>   *The Lord God will give him*
>
>   *the throne of his father David;*
>
> [33]*He will rule Jacob's house forever—*
>
>   *no end, ever, to his kingdom."*

[34]*Mary said to the angel, "But how? I've never slept with a man."*

[35]*The angel answered,*

> *The Holy Spirit will come upon you,*
>
>   *the power of the Highest hover over you;*
>
> *Therefore, the child you bring to birth*
>
>   *will be called Holy, Son of God.*

[36]*"And did you know that your cousin Elizabeth conceived a son, old as she is? Everyone called her barren, and here she is six months' pregnant!* [37]*Nothing, you see, is impossible with God."*

38And Mary said,

>*Yes, I see it all now:*
>*I'm the Lord's maid, ready to serve.*
>*Let it be with me*
>>*just as you say.*

Then the angel left her.

8. What was the first thing Gabriel said? Why do you think Mary was shaken?

9. What did Gabriel tell her about the Son who would be born to her? Find everything you can.

10. Do you see a difference between Mary's "How?" and Zechariah's "How?" If so, what?

11. How does Gabriel tell her Jesus will be conceived?

12. Read Deuteronomy 22:13-21. What was the punishment for a woman found to be unfaithful to her betrothed?

13. What was Mary's response to Gabriel? Why was this remarkable?

14. What is a challenging thing that God has asked or is asking of you? How did you or are you responding?

DAY 4

• •

The Greeting Scene

A pattern in Scripture is for God to zoom His camera in on the meeting and parting of friends. The greeting scene between Mary and Elizabeth is a famous one, and one that many artists and poets have attempted to capture. It is thrilling that God is so clearly meeting the needs of these two women. He is, as Mary says, "mindful of the humble estate of His servant." He knows our needs better than we do, He cares, and He is full of surprises. Mary hadn't told Elizabeth that she was pregnant with the Messiah, and since she was just a few days pregnant, she certainly wasn't showing. But Elizabeth knew. What a surprise Elizabeth's words must have been! What confirmation! And if Mary had had any doubts during her nearly one-hundred-mile walk to Elizabeth's home, if she had wondered if she had *really* seen Gabriel, or if she was having delusions of grandeur, then God made it clear that yes, this was *really* happening, and that she was, indeed, blessed among women.

Walter Wangerin wrote: "Faith is work. It is a struggle. You must struggle with all your heart.... And on the way, God will ambush you." I identify with Wangerin's play on words, for there have been times when I have been so surprised by God's response to my mustard seed of faith! Certainly it was a hard act of faith for Mary to travel one hundred miles alone to see Elizabeth, and she obviously expected some encouragement but, oh my, what an overwhelming scene!

15. Using the journalistic questions of who, what, why, where, and how, write down everything you can discover from Luke 1:39-40.

16. What two things happened to Elizabeth before she began to prophesy?

God knew Elizabeth's needs as well. She was elderly and had a husband who couldn't talk. How wonderful for her to have a strong, young woman come for an extended visit, a woman with whom God had also done the impossible.

17. Meditate on Luke 1:42.

    A. What are the first two blessings Elizabeth speaks to Mary?

    B. Put yourself in Mary's place. Do you think she was surprised Elizabeth knew? How do you think Elizabeth's words made her feel?

18. Meditate on Luke 1:43.

  A. How does Elizabeth show pleasure?

  B. Elizabeth could have been jealous, for she is just carrying John the Baptist, but instead, she shows humility and honor. Why do you think she wasn't jealous?

When a person is concerned with the praise of man, she tends to be jealous, but when she is concerned with the praise of God, she can truly rejoice for her friends' blessings, for she knows God has a plan for her too.

  C. Do you rejoice for your friends who are greatly blessed? Can you think of a time recently when you did or did not?

19. Meditate on Luke 1:44.

  A. What does Elizabeth tell Mary just happened?

  B. Why do you think John the Baptist leapt?

  C. Luci Shaw's poem, "Salutation" (at the beginning of chapter 12 in *The Friendships of Women)* makes a wonderful parallel between John the Baptist being excited to sense Jesus in Mary, and our sensing Jesus living in another person. ("And my heart turns over when I see Jesus in you.") Have you ever had the experience of meeting someone and knowing she was a believer before words confirmed it? If so, share why you thought so and how you felt.

  D. What do you think some of Elizabeth's feelings were and why?

20. Meditate on Luke 1:45.

  A. What does Elizabeth tell Mary?

B. What contrast has Elizabeth seen between Zechariah and Mary?

Zechariah is a godly man, but he was slower to believe. He responds beautifully to his discipline however, as evidenced by his song when his child is born.

C. How must these words have affirmed and encouraged Mary?

Action Assignment

E-mail, write, or call a friend in whom you have seen genuine faith, stepping out in some notable way. Tell her that you are inspired by her example and that you know God will bless her for believing Him.

DAY 5
. . . .

My Soul Doth Magnify the Lord

The richest friends you could ever find are worshipers of God. Mary was certainly that. In response to Elizabeth's prophecies, Mary sings her famous Magnificat. Jesus said that the mouth speaks what the heart is full of, and Mary's heart was certainly full of Scripture. Though Mary was probably a young teen, she certainly knew and loved the Word, for passages from Hannah's song, the Psalms, and the prophets create a spontaneous prayer that has gone down in history. By praying not only spontaneously but also Scripture, our prayers are kept from being trite or shallow. How much richer is Mary's prayer than if she had simply said, "Oh Lord I praise You. You are so wonderful and amazing!"

21. If you read chapter 11 of *The Friendships of Women*, what stood out to you?

22. Meditate on the Magnificat (Luke 1:46-53):

A. What is Mary's first response? (vs. 46-47) What does "magnify" mean?

B. What similarities do you see between the opening several verses of Mary's prayer and the opening several verses of Hannah's prayer in 1 Samuel 2?

C. List four reasons, according to Luke 1:48-49, that Mary is overwhelmed with praise.

D. Share briefly a time (recent if possible) when you were overwhelmed because you realized that the Almighty had been mindful of you.

E. What promise is in Psalm 103:17? Give evidence from the Magnificat that Mary knew this.

F. The Psalms, the prophets, and Jesus Himself (in the Sermon on the Mount) all spoke of a coming great reversal. Those who were not esteemed on earth may be great in heaven, yet those who were esteemed may not even be in heaven. Many poor will be rich, and many rich will be poor. The proud will be humbled, the humble, exalted. How do you see this great reversal in Luke 1:51-53?

G. It was common for the psalmists and prophets to recount God's promises and the fulfillments of those promises to Israel. How do you see Mary doing this in an abbreviated form in Luke 1:54-55?

H. I have always loved Mark Lowry's song, "Mary Did You Know?" Did Mary know that when she kissed her baby she was kissing the face of God? Did she know that the one she delivered would soon deliver her? Did she know that her baby boy would save her sons and daughters? Based on her Magnificat, how much do you think she understood?

PRAYER TIME

Cluster in groups of three or four. As Elizabeth affirmed Mary, affirm one another. Lift up a woman's name, and then have others give thanks for something they see praiseworthy in her. When you are done giving thanks for one another, magnify the Lord. Have as many as wish thank the Lord for a time when He was mindful of them, or for a way they have seen His holiness, mercy, or power.

Twelve

The Mentor Relationship

Have you ever driven in a thick fog? Often the only way you can drive and stay on the road is if there is a car ahead of you, keeping you, by its steady taillights, from going into the ditch. This is the picture author Win Couchman uses to describe the mentor relationship. A mentor is someone who is a little further down the road from you, who is going where you want to go, is doing it well, and gives you light for the path ahead.

Often the time we need light the most is in the dark storms of life. When our sixteen-year-old son became a prodigal, our family was in the midst of one of those storms. I remembered the example of Mary and how she traveled so far to see Elizabeth. So, in the same way, I traveled to Indiana, to spend one-on-one time with a woman who had mentored me when I was a baby Christian and whom I desperately needed again. Shirley had raised three children well, had experienced a prodigal, and whom, I knew, had light to give me. My time with her helped me immeasurably, and it wasn't long after, our own prodigal turned around dramatically. My mentor gave me light to get through the storm successfully.

So often we run to a peer when we have troubles. What are we thinking? How much wiser it is to run to a godly woman who has been there and done it well! Consider women who have trusted God in similar storms and have seen Him do amazing things.

DAY I

Blameless and Barren

Elizabeth had faced storms and trusted God. Even today, when a woman's whole identity is not defined by motherhood, infertility is still an enormous test of faith. The heartbreak is enormous. One woman shared:

I'm always, always, dwelling on it. Every month I hope my period won't come, and then I must bear the crushing disappointment when it does. For that week and the week following I think, *We will never, never have a baby of our own.* And then, from deep inside of me, hope springs up again, and climbs, as I think, *Maybe this month it will really happen!*

I sympathize with her pain, for my children are the delight of my life. But people today don't look upon infertile women with reproach, as they did in Elizabeth's day. Barren women then had to bear not only the sadness of not having a child, but also the cultural condemnation that they had missed their lives' calling, perhaps because of disobedience!

This, of course, was not God's point of view but man's. We know that God was pleased with Elizabeth, for we are told that she was upright in His sight (Luke 1:6). I love it that the English has two *B* words together: "blameless and barren." How much clearer could it be? Storms in our life are not necessarily due to sin but because God has a plan we cannot see.

The wisest, the most compassionate, and humblest people I know are those who have suffered yet, in that suffering, trusted God. These people make incredible mentors.

WARMUP

Think about an area where you have suffered. How did God comfort you in that particular storm?

In your private time with God, pray through Psalm 119:161-168. While you may not identify with the circumstances of "rulers persecuting you," you probably can identify with spiritual forces of darkness persecuting you. No matter the circumstances of your life, pray you will be like the psalmist who clung to God, praised Him in the storms, and loved His Word.

Rulers persecute me without cause,
*   but my heart trembles at your word.*

I rejoice in your promise
*   like one who finds great spoil.*

I hate and abhor falsehood
*   but I love your law.*

Seven times a day I praise you
*   for your righteous laws.*

Great peace have they who love your law,
*   and nothing can make them stumble.*

I wait for your salvation, O LORD,
*   and I follow your commands.*

I obey your statutes,
*   for I love them greatly.*

I obey your precepts and your statutes,
  for all my ways are known to you.

1. Meditate on Luke 1:6-7. Describe both the difficulty and the character of Elizabeth's life.

2. If you have struggled with infertility or are very close to someone who has, share something about the pain.

3. Meditate on 2 Corinthians 1:3-4.

   A. What can happen in an individual's life as a result of suffering?

   B. Think of a time when God comforted you in your suffering. How did He do it?

   C. Have you been able to comfort another with the comfort you received?

   D. What are some ways God comforted Elizabeth?

   E. What did she tell Mary in Luke 1:43? How had she learned that personally?

4. How might Elizabeth been particularly equipped to mentor Mary for the hard road that lay ahead? Consider the following circumstances Mary would face, and imagine how Elizabeth might have been able to prepare her:

   A. Joseph did not at first believe Gabriel's news. (Compare with Luke 1:18.)

B. Mary might have felt some reproach from the people of Nazareth. (Compare with Luke 1:25.)

C. Mary would be having her firstborn without mother or midwife to help. If she stayed for the birth of Elizabeth's baby, how might that have been helpful?

Matthew Henry comments that though Luke does not describe Mary being at the birth of John the Baptist, that doesn't mean she was not, for Luke does not tell us many things. "The probability," Henry writes, "is that she was there." It doesn't make sense that she would stay three months and leave just before she was needed the most.

5. What progression do you see that can come from tribulation according to Romans 5:5? How can you see this in Elizabeth?

6. See if you can discover from Luke 1 approximately where Elizabeth was in her pregnancy when Mary arrived and how long Mary stayed. Why do you think Mary stayed so long?

My discovery that Mary spent three months with Elizabeth was, "Three months! Perhaps someone should have given Mary a nudge about her manners!" I asked Win Couchman, who is a retreat speaker on the subject of cross-generational relationships what she thought about Mary's three-month visit. She told me that having a Filipino daughter-in-law has helped her to understand the story of Mary's visit to Elizabeth. Win said, "Lengthy visits and visits away from fiancé or husband seem so natural to her. And especially natural would be the visit between two pregnant relatives. There is an extremely open sharing between women in a family that I have been learning, to my delight, from this precious provincial woman. Her view of time is so different. Three months? A short visit."

Now, as I am growing in my appreciation of the value of mentors, I realize that God planned this lengthy visit to help Mary prepare for the dark and unique obstacles on the road ahead, including, I believe, giving birth to her firstborn in difficult circumstances.

7. How frequently do you extend hospitality to younger women? (For we are all older than someone!)

DAY 2

Elizabeth, Mary's Mentor

Elizabeth means "worshiper of God." We see this repeat in God's friendship pattern— the most valuable friends are worshipers of God, and Elizabeth lives up to her name. We are told she led a blameless life.

8. Write down the main point of each of the following passages to come up with a definition of "blameless."

    A. 1 John 1:6

    B. 1 John 1:9

    C. 1 John 1:10

    D. Philippians 1:9-11

    E. Philippians 2:14-15

    F. 2 Peter 3:13-14

9. Based on the above, describe a person who is living a "blameless life." Does it mean sinless? Why or why not? What does it mean?

10. What evidence do you find in the text of Luke 1 that Elizabeth was a worshiper of God?

11. How might have Elizabeth been able to prepare Mary to be a wife?

Mary must have watched with interest just how a godly couple related to each other in marriage. She and Joseph would not have the balm of a sexual relationship to soothe them during their first months of marital adjustment. Mary and Joseph had not used up their balm, but they would not be using it, as there were to be no sexual relations until after Jesus was born. Mary and Joseph were going to need, instead, the balms of kindness, tenderness, and trust in God. And I believe God built up this balm in Mary by providing her with a mentor, a devout older woman who showed respect and love for her husband.

12. How might have Elizabeth prepared Mary to be a mother?

How delightful it must have been to be with a friend who was pregnant and to know you were both carrying sons! I can picture them dying material blue together, sewing a layette, and talking all the time about how to rear boys! Perhaps they sharpened each other through their knowledge of prophecies concerning their sons.

And finally, before Mary headed back to Nazareth, I think she helped in the delivery of John the Baptist. She did not know, at this time, that she would be giving birth in a stable; but God knew, and I'm convinced He provided her with seeing a baby born, the umbilical cord tied and cut, and the baby washed and wrapped in swaddling clothes.

13. How might Elizabeth have been able to prepare Mary for the times ahead when God would not make sense?

Private Reflection:

Who are some of the women in your life who have trusted God in the storms of life and who might have something to teach you?

DAY 3

Mentoring Versus Discipleship

In discipling, you typically meet with someone and teach her how to do the spiritual disciplines that can be a vehicle of grace in her life. You teach her inductive Bible study skills, ways to pray effectively, ways to witness, and how to memorize Scripture.

Mentoring is much less formal than discipleship. It happens naturally, as you watch someone, picking up, almost by osmosis, how to discipline children, how to talk to your husband respectfully, how to not cheat your boss of a fair day's work, or how to be gracious, honest, and keep a reign over your tongue. You may pick up particular skills as well, such as how a soft answer can turn away wrath, how to make homemade soup, or how to keep your desk clutter free. You may certainly ask for training in something specific, but mentoring can happen without any particular training. It can happen in the workplace or the park, but often, it happens best in the home where you can get to know a woman in her natural surroundings.

The lesson on Titus 2, a familiar mentoring passage, will have some controversial questions, but controversy makes us dig to discover the truth. So before you are tempted to peek at any answers in the Leader's Helps, be sure you ponder and dig into Scripture on your own.

Perhaps the best known passage on women mentoring women is in Titus 2. Today we'll look at this carefully.

14. Meditate on the Titus 2 passage in the *New American Standard* version.

Older women likewise are to be reverent in their behavior, not malicious gossips nor enslaved to much wine, teaching what is good.

> A. What are two positive qualities a mentor should have, according to Titus 2, and what do you think is meant by each?

> B. What are two negative habits a mentor should not have? What insights do the descriptions give into each of these negative habits?

⁴so that they may encourage the young women to love their husbands, to love their children.

> C. What is a mentor to encourage the younger women to do?

> D. What are some ways a mentor might do this, other than simply telling her she should?

⁵to be sensible, pure, (H)workers at home, kind, being (I)subject to their own husbands, (J)so that the word of God will not be dishonored (footnotes added, mine).

> E. List the first two qualities we are to encourage in younger women. Who do you know who exemplifies these qualities, and why do you think of these particular women?

> F. What do you think it means to be "workers at home"?

The Greek word translated "workers" is literally "keepers," or "guards." This woman protects. Though it certainly includes protecting against chaos, cholesterol, and colds, it also goes beyond the body to the mind and soul. This woman is protecting against the corruption that can come in through the media, the internet, false teaching, or bad company. This woman is making the home a haven, protecting herself and her family against being so busy that they lose the reflective life, "the quiet life" we are instructed to live (1 Tim. 2:2).

G. Do you think "workers at home" means that a mother should not hold a job other than mothering? Support your answer scripturally, if you can.

H. How might you be a better "worker or keeper at home," even if you live by yourself?

I. To whom is a wife to be subject? What does this mean?

This is a "hot" potato and truly needs whole lessons to cover it in a way that is fitting with the truth of God. (In *A Woman of Confidence*, my updated guide on 1 Peter, I do this.) However, it is important to understand that God sees men and women as equals (co-heirs). He has ordained men to be servant-leaders in the home, loving and sacrificing for their wives, as Christ laid down His life for His Bride, the Church. The wife is commanded to honor him, to "fit in with his plans" as long as those plans are not in rebellion against God, that their marriage might be a Christian unity.

J. What reason is given at the close of verse 5 for a woman to embrace all of the above characteristics? Explain.

DAY 4

Mothers-in-Law and Daughters-in-Law

My sister Bonnie is a blithe spirit, energetic and cheerfully eager about each day, seldom heavy-hearted. The exception, which surprised us all, was the year following her mother-in-law's death. My sister was devastated. Seven years later, as Bonnie and I sat on the beach together, I asked her to tell me why she loved Lillian so much. Her words tumbled out, and even then, after so much time, tears welled up in my normally dry-eyed sister:

Everybody loved Lillian! Just being near her was a comfort and a lift. Her humor, her joy in life, her attentiveness to your thoughts and feelings, her quiet faith. Lillian spent three months living with us one time. My friends raised their eyebrows and said, "Three months? Three months with your mother-in-law in the same house?" But it wasn't a difficult time. It is a joyous, precious memory in our lives. It helped that she was sensitive to both my need for privacy and my need for help. She would take long walks. She would completely stay out of the kitchen during preparation time. She said two cooks was one too many—so instead she would talk to the kids. I liked that. Then, afterward, she would insist on cleaning up by herself. But I think I was drawn to her because of the way she loved me. I didn't feel like a daughter-in-law but like a beloved daughter. Her actions, her eyes, and her smile told me— but if I didn't know, she wasn't hesitant to express it. If she sensed I was troubled she would say, "I hope you know how very much I love you." ... I miss her so much.

It is also vital that daughters-in-law give their mothers-in-law a chance. I remember thinking as a newlywed that my mother-in-law should have it all together because she was so old. Now that I am a mother-in-law, I am so much more sympathetic. I was forty-four when John married Julie, and I was still very good at putting my foot in my mouth. Fortunately, John was quick to tell me, "You hurt Julie when you ..." But even though there were times I hurt her, times when I didn't make her feel valued, Julie responded with grace. Grace is not natural; when my mother-in-law hurt me, I wanted to withdraw. When I hurt Julie, instead of withdrawing, she gave me love. Because Julie gave me grace, today we are very close, and I truly see her, not as a daughter-in-law, but as a daughter.

15. As you review the book of Ruth, what evidence can you find that Naomi cared deeply about Ruth and showed her love, even though Ruth may not have been, at least initially, her "dream" daughter-in-law?

16. If you are a mother-in-law (or aunt) what are some ways you have shown genuine love toward your daughter-in-law (or niece)? How could you, with God's grace, improve?

17. What advice would you give mothers-in-law for having a good relationship with their daughters-in-law?

18. As you review the book of Ruth, what evidence can you find that Ruth cared deeply for Naomi and shared her heart with her, rather than holding her at arm's length?

19. If you are a daughter-in-law (or niece), what are some ways you have shown your mother-in-law (or aunt) that you care for her and are willing for her to be part of your life?

20. What advice would you give daughters-in-law for having a good relationship with their mothers-in-law?

DAY 5

Younger Women Initiate, Older Women Demonstrate Openness

An older women might be hesitant to reach out to a younger woman, wondering if she really has anything to offer. It is so helpful if the younger women, as Mary and as Ruth did, take the initiative. You might frighten her if you ask her to mentor you, but ask if you can spend some time with her in her home.

Older women can help by demonstrating openness. Talk to younger women at church, find out their children's names, and talk to them as well.

21. If you read chapter 12 of *The Friendships of Women*, what stood out to you?

22. Every woman should be mentoring and being mentored. Who are the mentors and the "mentees" in your life? How might you improve in this area?

23. What do you think you will remember about this lesson?

Pray through the last octrain of Psalm 119:

May my cry come before you, O Lord;
    give me understanding according to your word.

May my supplication come before you;
    deliver me according to your promise.

May my lips overflow with praise,
for you teach me your decrees.

May my tongue sing of your word,
for all your commands are righteous.

May your hand be ready to help me,
for I have chosen your precepts.

I long for your salvation, O LORD,
and your law is my delight.

Let me live that I may praise you,
and may your laws sustain me.

I have strayed like a lost sheep.
Seek your servant,
for I have not forgotten your commands.

PRAYER TIME

Cluster in groups of three or four. Have each woman lift up a confession or need of her heart, and then allow the others to support her. When there is a pause, another woman should lift up her need.

Thirteen

Reflections of Christ

Have you ever met someone, and before she could tell you that she was a believer, you knew? There was something in her spirit, her radiance, and her kindness that made you recognize the Spirit of the living God in her.

A principle of power found in 1 John is that as we practice the truths God has taught us, He becomes **complete** in us (1 John 2:5). Likewise, when we fail to practice these truths, the darkness becomes stronger in us. Read carefully what John Stott, a leading teacher in the Christian world, explains:

> Our love and our hatred not only reveal if we are in the light or in the darkness,
> but actually contribute to the light or darkness in which we already are.

We *can* become more like Christ. I am coming to understand, more and more, and with awe, what the apostle John meant when he said, "For we realize that our life in this world is actually His life lived in us" (1 John 4:17 PH). The beauty we see in Ruth, Jonathan, and Elizabeth is actually the beauty of God's Spirit, the Spirit of Jesus Christ. That same Spirit is available to you and me and will **grow** in us as we practice the principles He has taught and modeled. Let us review, this final week, some of the key threads from God's friendship pattern. If you practice them, you will see the transformation of Christ growing in you.

DAY I
....

Primary Thread: Worshiping God Instead of People

As women most of us have a natural gift for intimacy. Studies show our friendships are deeper, more enduring, and more plentiful than the friendships of men. This is our strength. Our weakness is that we have a tendency to depend on people instead of God.

Often the terror for women is isolation. But this is where sisters in Christ can be so different; we need to aspire to being worshipers of God, instead of worshipers of people. That will rid us of our Achilles' heel, and we will cherish our friends, not cling to them as if they were gods. If God calls us to be alone for a season, we will not panic but run to Him, as Elizabeth did for five months!

Sometimes God takes friends out of our life in order to help us worship Him alone. When Steve told me were going to leave Seattle, I sobbed out my misery to my sister Sally on the telephone. Sally said, "Dee, calm down. Do you know where your real home is?"

"Seattle!" I sobbed. "My friends are here, my church is here, my home is here."

"Your real home, Dee," my sister wisely said, "is in heaven. You are just passing through, and Seattle was a temporary tent stop." As Sally lifted my eyes beyond the horizons of this earth to my real home, I realized she was speaking the truth. The temporal things will pass away, and we need to place our feet securely on the solid rock of Jesus Christ. It's important to love our friends and to commit to them. But we need to depend on God because He's the only one who will never leave us. God taught me this through His friendship pattern, knowing how desperately I would need it when I became a young widow.

It should encourage us to see how Ruth, David, and Mary depended on God and found Him absolutely faithful. I have as well. He has truly become my Provider, Protector, and Confidante.

What is a worshiper? Remember the portrait of Mary of Bethany. A worshiper gives honor to Jesus with her teachable heart, devotion, obedience, and sacrifice. We see this in Mary the mother of Jesus, in Ruth, in truly, all of our models. Worshipers of God also make the very best friends. Out of the overflow of their hearts they bless others with their words and actions.

1. From the following passages, how can you see that Christ's trust was in God, rather than in people?

    A. John 2:23-25

    B. 1 Peter 2:23

2. What is the root sin of homosexuality? (Rom. 1) What do you remember from Rachel's story? Has this study impacted you in any way on this subject? If so, how?

3. What is relational idolatry? Christy told her story and how she was set free. What do you remember? What are the signs that someone may be in bondage?

4. What evidence can you give that each person was a worshiper of God instead of a worshiper of people? What evidence can you give for each being an amazing friend?

    A. Ruth

        1. Worshiper? (Consider both her words and the risks she took, based on her faith that God could be trusted.)

        2. Amazing friend?

    B. Jonathan

        1. Worshiper? (How did you see Jonathan zealous for God's reputation?)

        2. Amazing friend?

    C. Mary

        1. Worshiper?

        2. Amazing friend?

    D. Elizabeth

        1. Worshiper?

        2. Amazing friend?

5. Reflect on praying through Psalm 119. Was this helpful to you in increasing your strength in worshiping God? If so, why? How might you continue praying the Psalms?

6. As you are still before the Lord, what does He impress on your heart about applying this thread from God's friendship pattern?

DAY 2

Greeting Scenes

Remember Isabel's thoughts upon meeting Sybil in London? "I tend to be solitary and had not realized my own need to interact with someone deeply. I began to catch on that God was giving me the gift of a friend."

How vital it is that we be alert to the Holy Spirit! Often we are so programmed, even what we feel is God's agenda, that we work at cross-purposes with Him. My pastor's wife, Allie Jo, is a true servant of God, and her day is *fully programmed* to be an excellent wife and mother and to minister to those in the congregation. Her little heels click rapidly across the floor as she hurries from one task to another. One cold winter day, after she had given her high-school home-schooled daughter an assignment in math, she took their dog for a quick walk up the block. She noticed that the "For Sale" sign on a neighbor's house had been replaced with a "Sold" sign. Just then a woman who was also walking her dog came toward the house. Tentatively Allie Jo took a risk, asking, "Are you our new neighbor?"

Marsha said, "Though I am normally very reserved, I was so desperate for a friend I took the plunge and invited this sweet woman in for coffee."

Allie Jo hesitated. Her daughter was waiting for her. Her day was full. It was cold and their little dog couldn't be outside long. Yet....she thought, *How often do you have an opportunity like this?* Fortunately, Allie Jo was sensitive to the Spirit and accepted. And, as you may have guessed, God had definitely orchestrated this, for Marsha was a sister in Christ who was praying for fellowship, and she and Allie Jo discovered they had so many unusual bonds in common.

Marsha had been actively praying for a friend, something we all need to do. Because God knows our needs better than we do, greeting scenes are often dramatic reminders that He is very involved in orchestrating our friendships. Pray for friends who are rich in Christ, or for mentors, "mentees," or those who are open to Him. Be willing to take a risk when you sense God may be leading.

7. Give examples from Christ's life that show how He was willing to interrupt His schedule and minister to someone who came across His path.

8. Each of the following individuals took a risk in reaching out to someone. Describe what they might have known about that individual and then describe the greeting scene.

    A. Jonathan

        1. What did he know about David? (1 Sam. 17)

        2. Describe the greeting scene and the risks Jonathan took.

B. Ruth

    1. What did Ruth know about Naomi? (You may need to read between the lines in Ruth 1:1-15.)

    2. What risk do you see Ruth taking? Why?

C. Boaz

    1.What did Boaz know about Ruth?

    2. Describe their greeting scene. What are some ways Boaz "showed himself friendly" to Ruth?

D. Mary

    1. What did Mary know about Elizabeth?

9. Do you have friends who really encourage you spiritually because they are truly worshipers, giant slayers, or poets?

10. How prayerful and alert are you to reaching out to friends who are rich in Christ? How open are you if someone makes an overture toward you to consider if God might be in it?

11. How might you apply this thread from God's friendship pattern?

DAY 3

Sensitivity to the Holy Spirit

Sensitivity to the Spirit is needed not only in finding friends, but also in being one. One of the characteristics of a fool is that he is all about himself. He doesn't stop and listen to God, he just does what he thinks is right in his own heart. How different David was from Saul because of David's sensitivity to the Spirit. Remember David's Psalm 5? He says:

> *In the morning, O LORD, you hear my voice; in the morning I lay my requests before you and wait in expectation.*
> Psalm 5:3

163

If we would stop and ask God to plan our day and put His desires in our heart, our friendships would be dramatically enriched.

As women, most of us have been blessed by God with the gift of intuition. There are times when we're going to be wrong, but if we check our "hunches" with God's Word, we will be wise to move ahead when something seems "good to the Holy Spirit and to us" (Acts 15:28).

In order to use your gift of intuition wisely in friendship, let me ask you: Are you reading through the Bible regularly? Are you memorizing Scripture regularly? The Holy Spirit never conflicts with the Word, so this must be the starting point.

We know, for example, that Scripture exhorts us to encourage one another, to carry one another's burdens, and to speak the truth in love. But knowing when and to whom to apply these principles involves an intertwining of intuition with Holy Spirit power. For example, I just had my first birthday without Steve. How comforted I was by the women who intuitively knew it would be a hard day and obeyed the Holy Spirit in finding ways to bless me. Jayne sent fragrant flowers; Bonnie took me to lunch; and Kathy helped me do an extreme makeover of a room in my cottage. This birthday, they intuitively knew, needed an extra dose of love. They also knew God's Word is clear that we are to bind up the broken-hearted, and they did so.

One of the hardest things to do is to wait on God, but we certainly see this as well. Elizabeth spent five months in seclusion before God brought Mary across her path. Ruth had to wait for Naomi to respond to her love, and David had to wait years for God to remove Saul from his life. None of them forced God's hand but waited, trusting.

12. Describe what Jesus did before he chose the twelve disciples. (Luke 6:12-16)

13. Review how these women showed sensitivity to the Spirit and, in so doing, were a great blessing to a friend.

    A. Mary of Bethany (Mark 14:3-9)

    B. Ruth (Consider why Ruth was able to stay with Naomi after Naomi had sent her back four times and how Ruth was able to follow Naomi's risky plan.)

    C. Jonathan (See particularly, 1 Sam. 23:14-18.)

14. What evidence can you give that Mary and Elizabeth were immersed in the Scriptures? Sensitive to the Spirit?

15. Consider:

    A. How immersed are you in God's Word through study, memorization, and meditation?

B. How good a listener are you to the Holy Spirit? Do you practice being still before Him? Are you willing to drop your plans if you sense He is leading?

DAY 4

Unfailing Love

Naomi prayed that God would show Ruth unfailing love (Ruth 1:8), and Jonathan said to David, "Show me unfailing kindness like that of the Lord" (1 Sam. 20:14).

We are living in a time of impermanence and easy good-byes. It takes discipline to show unfailing love when a friend needs a great deal of help, moves away, or hurts you with unkind words. But how like Christ, who shows us His faithfulness morning by morning, we become if we can show steadfast kindness in these situations!

When Steve died, whether they wanted it or not, all my friends faced a test. I was shocked that I didn't even hear from some. I know how it can be hard to know what to say, and I do forgive them, for I know I have been faithless too. But I also now understand how, if I haven't been there for someone when she needed me the most, that she might be hesitant to keep me in her closest circle. Others showed unfailing love like that of the Lord: They wrote long letters filled with special memories of the man I loved, they flew across the country to be at his funeral, and instead of asking me, "Are you better now?" gave me the time I needed to grieve.

16. How does Lamentations 3:22-23 describe the love of the Lord? How have you experienced this from Him? Be specific.

17. Have you assessed your friendships? What friends would feel rightfully let down if you were not there for them in their time of need? To whom is the Spirit telling you to be true?

18. In order to give unfailing love, we need to be filled with grace, for our human friends will all let us down sooner or later. How did Naomi let Ruth down, and how did Ruth give grace? What could you learn from her that might be applicable in your life right now?

19. In order to be like Christ and the models in whom we have seen Him reflected, consider: How will you discipline yourself to remain true to your real connections? How will you respond if a close friend lets you down?

Part of unfailing love means that we do not withhold good from our friends when it is in our power to give it. Sometimes that means being willing to share our heart, not holding someone at arm's length. After her night with Boaz, Ruth told Naomi "everything." Jonathan and David bared their souls to each other, and Elizabeth didn't tone down her ecstasy in seeing Mary.

20. What pattern do you see repeated in Ruth 3:5 and 1 Samuel 20:4? What can you learn from this?

21. What examples did you see from our models of them verbally affirming each other?

22. How willing are you to make yourself vulnerable with your closest friends, telling them how you are really doing spiritually? How willing are you to verbally affirm them?

DAY 5

Parting Scenes

God zoomed His camera in on parting scenes between Ruth and Naomi and then again with David and Jonathan. As we watch them weep and cling to each other, we understand Shakespeare's words, "Parting is such sweet sorrow."

Likewise, Scripture shows us that Christ did not shrink from saying good-bye to those He loved. He began saying good-bye very early in His three-year ministry, warning them that He would be crucified. His words "Do not let your hearts be troubled" (John 14:1) remind me of Jonathan's parting words to David.

Words and emotions that are expressed in parting scenes come to our remembrance again and again. Parting scenes, though painful, are not wasted sadness. Since the original edition of this book, I have said good-bye to both my father and my husband. When I went to be with my dad at his deathbed, I read to him from a little journal I'd written and given to him on a Father's Day five years previous. It was filled with reasons I loved him. (He kept it on his desk.) One of the things I wrote was: "Dad—whenever I flew home, you were always at the gate." (This was in the days when you could still go to the gate to meet someone.) "I'd see your face searching for me, and then you'd see me and laugh, opening your arms for our great hug." The very last words I spoke to my dad on this earth, and which I know he heard, were, "Dad—please, please— be at the gate."

23. If you read the final chapter in *The Friendships of Women*, what stood out to you?

24. What do you remember from the parting scenes with Naomi and her daughters-in-law and with David and Jonathan?

25. What do you remember about "small parting scenes"?

26. How will you specifically apply this thread to your life?

27. List three things that you think you will always remember from this study. Why? What will you do with them?

My Parting Scene with You

The Lord has taught me some profound truths about friendship, and I hope that His teachings have flowed through me to you, my reader, and now my friend. So we are bound together in His truth and in His Spirit. It's painful to close this book; it's hard to say good-bye, but I am encouraged by C. S. Lewis's great shout, "REMEMBER! CHRISTIANS NEVER SAY GOOD-BYE!" I will meet every one of you who has personally trusted Christ for her salvation one day, in eternity! So I ask you to go in peace and to practice, as I will, God's friendship pattern.

In His Unfailing Love, Dee

PRAYER TIME

Cluster in groups of three or four and give specific thanks for the things you have learned from the Lord in this study.

Leader's Helps

Hints for the Leader:

Be a facilitator rather than a teacher

- If questions are directed to you, direct them back to the group.
- Encourage the shyer members by calling upon them when their facial expression shows they have something to share—"Annie, did you have a thought?"
- If you have a monopolizer, pray, and decide if you might need to talk to her privately, gently encouraging her to often hold back and see if the shyer women might speak up.
- When they are going on a rabbit trail, bring them gently back to the lesson.
- If they are getting sloppy about homework, call the more mature members and ask them to set an example.

Be a shepherd

- Affirm them through individual e-mails and phone calls so they know you truly do appreciate them.
- Begin and end on time.
- Reach out to the hurting through cards and visits.
- Encourage them in prayer—both in group and out—and to "pray" their requests.
- Plan a few social get togethers. At one, have them bless one another as Elizabeth did with Mary.
- Let absentees know they are missed.

Instructions for Blessing Time

- The facilitator should lift up the name of one of the women present, then three or four may affirm her. Then the facilitator lifts up the name of each woman, and the affirmation continues.
- Consider Elizabeth's model and how she affirmed Mary's faith. Look for godly characteristics and examples of faith and trust.

One: From Girlhood On, Gifted for Intimacy

3. Naomi lost her home, her husband, her dreams of godly daughters-in-law (for, though Ruth would eventually come to the one true God, she, at the time, like Orpah, worshiped the god of the Moabites—Chemosh), her hope of grandchildren (at that time both girls were barren), and her sons. Note the words "famine," "barrenness," "empty," and "Mara" in the first chapter.

4. She wept at the thought of leaving Naomi, she seemed to understand that Naomi's rejection of her was not personal, but based on her own pain. Though Naomi sends her back four times (count them!), Ruth persists, making her amazing commitment in Ruth 1:16-17. When Naomi still does not appreciate Ruth, Ruth does not give up. She doesn't give Naomi a sermon, but stands by her hurting friend and weeps with her, dividing her pain.

6. Hear from several. We show we are really paying attention when we ask questions, when we affirm, repeating part of what has been said, when we show, by nonverbal cues, that we appreciate what has been said. Really listening to one another, and building on it through questions, affirmations, or additions, rather than just waiting for our turn to talk, is key to taking one another higher.

13. Ruth is committing herself not only to Naomi, but to Naomi's God. How did Ruth know that God was reliable in the face of such a negative testimony from Naomi? It could be that Ruth remembered the way Naomi used to be, but also, it had to be that the Spirit of God was drawing Ruth.

14. We often think of what a wonderful friend Jonathan was to David, but David was also a great friend to Jonathan. Jonathan seemed to have a heart for God, despite his father's negative role model, and it may very well be that God, in His mercy, caused Jonathan to be drawn to David.

15. God used Gabriel to give Mary a huge clue that it would be good to go spend time with Elizabeth. These three months with Elizabeth were so much a part of God's plan that I believe His Spirit also propelled her!

PRAYER TIME

You may want to have three or four women provide a model here. Choose women who you know will keep their sentences short and simple. Or, you can have them act out the script provided.

Two: Unleashing Our Gift

2. Learning to observe is a vital skill—and you may have beginners. Help them help each other if this is new. For example, look at a Bible map and talk about the significance of Bethany being so close to Jerusalem. Talk about each guest and how they might have been feeling.

3. Teach them to ask questions and dig for answers, such as "What is nard?" "How much was a pint worth?" Cross-references will help them find answers. You can also introduce those who use the internet to biblegateway.com—a free resource that will help them see the passage in many translations, cross-references, and commentaries. However, without any additional resources or even cross-references, they should be able to see that:

Mary brought a pint of pure nard

Nard is an expensive perfume

She poured it on Jesus' feet

She wiped His feet with her hair

The house was filled with the fragrance of the oil

From the context, they can also see

A party was being held—so she had an audience

Her brother, who had been raised from the dead, was watching

Martha was serving while Mary was worshiping

The nard was worth three hundred denarii (a year's wages)

She causes a scene and receives criticism

Jesus defends her again

Jesus says she did it to prepare Him for His burial

8. An agreement to keep confidences within the group would be valuable.

15.A. Not only did Jonathan realize he would have to send his best friend away, he realized fully the kind of man his father was.

Three: The Darker Side of Being Crazy-Glued

2.E. Like the idols, they are blind, deaf, and powerless. Without the one true God, we are dead spiritually and can do nothing of eternal worth.

Four: Relational Idolatry

2.A. As a leader, be willing to lead the way by making yourself vulnerable. Share the pain of the bondage of a lie, or an addiction, or jealousy—and also the joy of being set free. How did freedom come?

5. They admitted their sin, they got help, and they separated from each other.

16.A. Myth: You may be gay and you don't know it. Experimenting with the same sex will help you to know.

> Before maturity, there is a natural attraction to the same sex for everyone. If you experiment, you can be stunted, instead of moving on to maturity. This is a dangerous suggestion.

B. Myth: If you have a predisposition toward homosexuality this is the way you must always be.

> Everybody has a predisposition toward some kind of sin, and everyone can, in Christ, be set free. That is His promise in John 8:32—you shall know the truth and the truth shall set you free.

C. Myth: It is not loving to tell someone that the practice of homosexuality is wrong. The Bible tells us not to judge.

On the contrary, it is unloving to encourage anyone in any sin. Sin leads to bondage and repentance to freedom. Judgment has to do with feeling superior. It is important for each person to realize they too are sinners. Realizing that, we must speak the truth in love, and God says the practice of homosexuality is not His plan.

D. Myth: David and Jonathan were homosexuals, and God was pleased with them.

They were knit together in soul, not in body. Some do not understand how intimacy is possible without a sexual relationship, but it is.

18. She admitted her sin, got help, and separated from her object of worship.

21.G. True repentance means admitting your sin and doing a U-Turn. Then you are emptied. But it is also vital to ask God to fill you with the Spirit, and to draw near to Him through worship and study.

Five: Naomi—A Female Job

1.C.5) Many commentators believe that God was looking for repentance, and Elimelech tried to get around him. We can only surmise, but we can see that Moab was a detestable land of idol worship, and Elimelech led his family into spiritual peril by moving there,much as Lot did when he moved to Sodom.

5. Though both Job and Naomi are in pain, and confess openly of the burden God has laid on them, they never curse Him, but speak of Him with reverence—they know He is powerful, wise, and holy. Both refer to Him at times as "The Almighty" (Job 24:1, Ruth 1:21), but also as the one who knows them (Job 23:10), who is their faithful source of mercy (Ruth 1:8-9), and whom they dare not stand against. They live in repentance rather than in rebellion (Job 1:1; 1:5; 42:6.) Many see Naomi's return to Bethlehem as a form of repentance. We cannot know that, but we see nothing in her attitude of rebellion—only sorrow at the burden God has allowed her to bear.

7. The chapter begins with famine and judgment—now, at the end, there is the hope of food and mercy: "arriving in Bethlehem as the barley harvest was beginning."

8. He reminded God of His promises—not that God forgets, but He loves it when His children remember. God's Word is His bond, and when we pray through His promises, we know we are praying truth.

27. He doubled everything except Job's children. However, truly, Job's children were doubled as well, for those who died were alive in heaven.

29. Naomi knew Boaz was their "kinsman-redeemer," a man that, according to Levitical law, should care for her, as the widow of his near relative. Naomi sees that God has not forgotten either her or her dead, for this means that her late husband's name may be carried on through Boaz. Naomi is actually the one Boaz would have ordinarily married, but Naomi chooses to have it be Ruth. Her testimony here is a positive one of God's goodness, leading, and care. No doubt Naomi was still in great pain, but she is testifying to God's goodness.

30.A. Boaz buys the land back—and Ruth and Naomi will live on it. Obed will inherit it.
B. Naomi's late husband's name will be carried on through Boaz, through Obed.

C. When they pray Ruth will be like Rachel and Leah; they are praying for fertility.

These women, together, "built up the house of Israel." The second prayer is quite bold, asking that their descendants will be famous in Bethlehem. The third, relating to Perez, probably is asking that the family line will be significant—as was the family line of Perez. (He is mentioned in Matthew in the genealogy of Christ.)

Six: Ruth—A Woman Friend

2.A. Naomi: **Go back to Moab.**

Ruth? I'm coming—all the way to Bethlehem. And I'm staying!

B. Naomi: **I do not have value anymore. No man would want me, and even if he did, I can't conceive anymore. I'm empty, worthless, I have nothing to give.**

Ruth? You are so valuable to me. I don't count worth on the basis of marital status or the ability to have children, but on if you love well. And oh, Naomi, you have loved me well. You treated me (and called me) not "daughter-in-law" but daughter. You are so different from the women of Moab. You have everything to give me.

C. Naomi: **I am not going to be pleasant to be around. Call me Mara.**

Ruth? You are hurting. And who wouldn't be? But I remember when you were pleasant, and I am going to stand by your side and restore you to the sweet Naomi that I remember. I am also not going to take your bitterness personally. I know that hurt people hurt people.

D. Naomi: **I'm not going to tell you to trust my God. He has dealt severely with me.**

Ruth? But I do trust your God. Thy God, Naomi, will be my God. (How did Ruth know this? I can only imagine that God's Spirit bore witness to her, and that, perhaps, she saw a difference in Naomi from the women of Moab—especially before Naomi was in high tide grief.)

8. This is important—hear from as many who desire to share.

18. (Malachi 2)

A. They have profaned their covenant to God, which includes their covenant to their wives.

B. They have married foreign women, casting aside their wives.

C. It is still church as usual! They are bringing sacrifices to the temple.

D. After this travesty, the men are angry with God for not receiving their sacrifices! They have been faithless to the wives of their youth, to their companions, to the one they were in covenant with. They have ripped apart the oneness God gave, and they have yoked with unbelievers, so they will raise ungodly children.

E. He hates divorce, and he hates the cover-up that the perpetrators of the divorce are attempting.

F. The address is to the perpetrator, not to the victim. May we stop, as a church, heaping shame on the victim!

Seven: Taking Risks

1.A. Ruth's risks: Leaving Moab, possibly remaining single for the rest of her life, promising to stay with Naomi until death, committing herself to Naomi's God, people, and to Naomi herself. After Naomi is unresponsive, she risks going out to glean in an unknown farm. She risks making herself vulnerable with Boaz, risks going into him and uncovering his feet, and risks telling him of her need.

   B. Blessed by God: godly friends, husband, a child who will become the grandfather of David and ancestor of Christ. A book in the Bible named after her. Loved by the people of Bethlehem.

   C. Naomi is restored to faith in God and to a family.

   D. They prayed fervently for her, and those prayers were answered magnificently in the birth of Obed.

   E. A woman of excellence.

   F. Marriage. You may want to point out that this doesn't necessarily mean women should take the initiative with men in dating or marriage, for this is also symbolic. Boaz is a Christ-figure, has drawn Ruth to himself, but she must respond in faith.

10.A. A coating of glaze makes an earthen pot look beautiful, but it is still an earthen pot. Charming words can make you think someone is wonderful, when, in fact, they may harbor an evil motive in their heart.

Eight: Best Friends

1. Our soul is knit to another and we love her (or him) as we love ourselves.

3.A. They both had faith that God could do the impossible.

   B. They both had difficult family situations.

23.A. Jesus prayed all night before choosing His disciples. Though the purpose of Christ was greater here than friendship, still, often our closest friends end up being partners in ministry, or at least, impacting our own ministries. How important to pray and be alert to whom God is choosing for us in friendship.

   B. Jesus had twelve close friends, but then He also had a more intimate circle. We may, as well.

   C. Even His closest friends let Him down, and ours will as well. That is why God must be our Solid Rock.

Nine: Unfailing Love

2. God loved us enough to adopt us as His children. This means we have been adopted into a family that includes many brothers and sisters, whom we should see as such. It also means that just as children have characteristics of their earthly parents, so we have characteristics of our heavenly Father. The heart of 1 John is that as we walk in those characteristics (light, love, truth, compassion) they become stronger in us.

4.D. All make an appeal to giving grace or mercy to a brother or sister. God longs for harmony in His family.

7. This command is narrower—it is for loving our brothers and sisters within the body of Christ.

15.A. He was taking off his "princely garments" and giving them to David, communicating to David that he was turning his right to be king over to him.

   B. When a new king, outside of the family, came to power, often the former king's children were killed so there would be no threat to the throne. Though David would not have initiated that, others might have carried that out.

The next lesson is long, and I would advise, if you have an extra week, to do three days in one week and then finish the following week.

Ten: Roses and Alligators

10. There are many more verses about fools in Scripture, and you may want to encourage them to do a study, using their concordance. There is a difference between being foolish and being a fool, so they should concentrate on the word "fool" rather than "foolish." A fool is hardened—and his life is all about himself. Because he thinks he is never wrong, he will become angry when confronted, he will not listen, and he will repeat his folly.

11. David did not flee until Saul showed a pattern of destruction. But when David saw a pattern, he fled. He also forgave Saul from his heart. The discussion may come up— how do you flee if it is a husband, a child, or a parent? First Corinthians 7:10 urges a woman married to an unbeliever to stay with him. But if she does separate (according to the next verse) she is not to divorce him. The implication is that sometimes separation is necessary. If her mate is not a fool, the pain of separation may bring him to his senses. He may agree to getting help. If he is a fool, he will persist in his folly, and either divorce her or give her, in all probability, scriptural grounds for divorce. If the person is a parent or a child, again, boundaries may be necessary. You may need to insist they get help and show the fruit of a changed life before close contact resumes.

22.C. He was willing to work as a hired servant instead of as a son.

Eleven: God Knows Your Needs Better than You Do

2. What commonalities?

   A. Luke 1:7 and Matthew 1:19

   Both were married to righteous godly men

   B. Luke 1:18-20 and Matthew 1:19-21

   Both men had trouble, at first, believing, whereas the women believed immediately. God helped each man to believe.

   C. Luke 1:13 and Luke 1:31

   Both women had "miracle" pregnancies, announced by Gabriel, and had sons named by God.

D. Luke 1:25 and Luke 1:48

Both endured reproach from their communities, and both had their reproach taken away.

E. Luke 1:57-58 and Luke 2:6-7; Luke 2:16-19

Both, at the birth of their sons, experienced the rejoicing and wonder of others around them.

It is also true the both of their sons died martyrs' deaths. We do not know, however, if Elizabeth was alive when her son John was murdered.

10. Zechariah was doubting, asking for confirmation. Mary was curious as to how God was going to do it. She believed He would—she wondered how.

15. Who? Mary to the home of Elizabeth and Zechariah.

Where? Look at a Bible map and approximate the distance Mary had to travel.

How? We can only speculate—she may have walked, ridden a donkey, or traveled with someone going that way.

When? She made haste—so, right away. Did she talk to Joseph before she left—did she know he didn't believe? We don't know. She was going for a long time. She knew Elizabeth was in her sixth month, and Matthew Henry thinks it is probably that she planned, and did stay for the birth of Elizabeth's baby in order to help. She knew, therefore, she'd be gone at least three months—so I think she would have first talked to her betrothed.

Why? I believe she pondered Gabriel's words and sensed God wanted her to go.

Twelve: The Mentor Relationship

2. If you know of a woman in your group who has struggled with this, ask her, ahead of time, if she'd be willing to share, just for a few minutes, on why it is so painful and how others have either increased or decreased her pain.

3.D. What a comfort Mary must have been, for she could so understand so much about Elizabeth's experience. What a comfort the Holy Spirit was in giving Elizabeth that amazing prophecy. And Zechariah, after having been disciplined, responded in a way that made you realize that Elizabeth had the comfort of a very godly husband and father.

14. Meditate on the Titus 2 passage in the *New American Standard* version.

Older women likewise are to be reverent in their behavior, not malicious gossips nor enslaved to much wine, teaching what is good.

A. Reverent—respectful and God-fearing. Teaching what is good. Most teaching occurs through modeling, and what is good? Justice, mercy, and walking humbly with our God are good places to start! (Micah…)

B. Gossip is malicious according to one definition of the Hebrew word: "rolling to pieces." If the person you are talking to is not involved in the problem, then you are rolling another person to pieces. The word *enslaved* is key—and could certainly apply to more habits than just having too much wine.

⁴so that they may encourage the young women to love their husbands, to love their children.

    C. Love husbands and children.

    D. Again, modeling is vital. A woman friend also can help her friend see things she might have been blind to—good qualities in her husband or children. She might also help a younger woman understand that men, truly, are different, and shouldn't be expected to react and respond like her women friends.

⁵to be sensible, pure, ⁽ᴴ⁾workers at home, kind, being ⁽ᴵ⁾subject to their own husbands, ⁽ᴶ⁾so that the word of God will not be dishonored.

    G. Do you think "workers at home" means that a mother should not hold a job other than mothering? Support your answer scripturally, if you can.

The reasons for cautions to mothers working outside the home are based more on the practicalities of obeying all the commands to parents than any black and white scriptural commands. The Proverbs 31 woman seemed to do it all, though she is actually a "composite" ideal woman. But on the side of staying at home when the children need you most, it is true that men are exhorted to be providers (1 Tim. 5:8) and that all are exhorted to be content with a simple life materially. How can we train our children to live a quiet life when we are not? How can we train our children when they rise up, when they walk by the way, and when they lie down (Deut. 6:7) if we aren't there? In these last days, there is more, not less, to protect them from, and mothering truly is a full-time career. Having said that, we have great freedom in Christ, and each of us will answer to Him for the priorities we choose. When our children were teens, my husband chose to take care of them on the weekends I traveled and spoke, and we felt God's blessing on that choice, despite some wagging tongues. At Steve's funeral, our daughter Beth said, "I liked the weekends Mom was gone so I could have a father/daughter weekend." The crowd laughed, and I felt like Elizabeth when she said: "God has taken away my disgrace among the people!" Be careful about judging, but look prayerfully at your own priorities.

    J. What reason is given at the close of verse 5 for a woman to embrace all of the above characteristics? Explain.

15. Notice Naomi's prayer for Ruth (and Orpah) in the opening. Then see, once Naomi began to heal, how diligently she planned, putting feet to that prayer! She actually was the one that Boaz was obligated to care for, but she sent Ruth in her place.

18. Notice how Ruth not only committed her whole life to Naomi, but followed through, even when Naomi said, "I've come back empty." She also didn't hold Naomi at arm's length but told her "everything." Obviously Boaz and Ruth included Naomi in their family after marriage.